Legal

--From a Declaration of Principles Jointly Adopted by a Committee of the American Bar Association and a Committee of Publishers and Associations.

Under no circumstances should any material in this book be used or considered as an offer to sell or a solicitation of any offer to buy an interest in Infrastructure Upgrade, Inc.® and/or in any individual company, any investment fund or any individual in this book.

The views and opinions expressed herein are those of the author alone and do not reflect the views of any university, employers, former employers and/or their affiliates.

Under no circumstances should any material in this book be construed as an endorsement for and/or against any existing (or former) political candidates in elected office.

Thank You

This book is dedicated to my immediate family. It is also a tribute to those that were instrumental in my growth.

The following mentors are to be acknowledged:

Denis Lau, Steve Kolt and Ron Mun.

2009 Photo of Matthew Myers at the University of Hawaiʻi.

Table of Contents

Introduction

I wrote Volume 2 of this trilogy during between yearlong house renovations in Connecticut. The 2nd volume combines micro and macroeconomic analysis and technical professional experiences along with personal advancements. Volume 3 is being finalized.

Volume 3 will provide insights into the photo above!

Funding Projects with Expected and Unexpected Outcomes

Calculated experimentation is critical to business growth, research and development in conjunction with government and military spending. It is not an accident that many of the great inventions of the 19th and 20th centuries were accomplished through trial and error. A research and development team is not a cursory business outlier. It is central to any undertaken operation. The same is true for government-funded research, which produced technologies that resulted in the space program and computer based networks. These technologies were developed and funded initially in part to support the U.S. armed forces and their operations. However, modern satellite technologies (and their associated companies like SpaceX®) are the modern beneficiaries of the research that was funded by the government decades ago. The modern manifestation of connecting multiple computers together on a single network based on specific IP addresses and protocols is exhibited in companies like Amazon® and eBay® that are able to engage in commerce and auctions through a seamless interface.

Research and development (R&D) requires a substantial amount of upfront investment. Hedge funds and activist investors typically argue against the short-term monetary benefits of R&D. This argument benefits their self-interest, but is not a shrewd long-term strategy. Corporations peak at some point in their lifecycle. If they haven't engaged in innovations they decline and are acquired; or they must invest in other companies in order to remain viable. Yahoo!® is a classic example of this decline. Even with its acquisition of companies like Alibaba®, it was unable to remain innovative, lost market share and revenues and was ultimately acquired.

The funding of an island's restoration is used as an example of the critical nature of funding projects that have unexpected outcomes. The unanticipated results of this research have benefits for insurance companies, housing developers and other multi-national corporations.

Why is this the case?

Companies can use this government-funded research to reduce their bottom line costs and increase profitability. The mudslides that occurred near Santa Barbara, California are a prime example of how the research conducted on erosion on Kahoʻolawe, Hawaiʻi can be utilized to make insurance companies and banks more profitable; and communities safer and more proactive in their approach to dealing with exceptional climate events and natural disasters.

When I worked at the State of Hawaiʻi Department of Health, Clean Water Branch I designed a project in partnership with the United States Environmental Protection Agency (EPA), U.S. Geological Service (USGS), U.S. Military – Navy (for unexploded ordinances) and the Kahoʻolawe Island Reserve Commission (KIRC).

To understand Kahoʻolawe is to know it's complex history as a military bombing range, predated by its limited habitation by Polynesians in its earlier history. The island is largely barren from severe loss of vegetation from bombing and invasive animals. During flash floods huge volumes of soil and suspended sediment flow into the ocean. Nearly 2 million tons of sediment is lost from the islands surface during the course of a year. As a consequence, it is an excellent location to conduct geological research.

Kahoʻolawe is the eighth largest of the main Hawaiian Islands located 11.2 km southwest of Maui. It is approximately 1.03 million years old and is 17km long by 11km wide (an area of 117km^2). Its highest point is at Pu'u Moa'ulanui, elevation 452m. It is a single shield volcano with a 5km wide caldera and a north rift zone that contains Lua Makika crater and the summit area of Pu'u Moa'ulanui. Kahoʻolawe lies at the apex of a natural wind tunnel and wind speeds range from 8 to 50km per hour. Storm events may produce higher wind speeds and gusts that exceed this range. This is due in part to little to no vegetation or tree coverage, and/or significant mountain ranges on the island. Ranges in temperature in the proposed project site are from 19°C to 26°C, slope from 0° to 7° and elevation from sea level to 20m, and 350m to 400m.[1] Rainfall is 60 cm/year (25 in/year) and streams are ephemeral.[2] Storm events that exceed this volume are common causing mudslides and

---

[1]KIRC. May 6. 2005.
[2]Id.

extreme flash flooding in short periods of time. These flash flood events are extremely dangerous and have the potential to sweep away large volumes of soil and vegetation. In areas of high population density houses and business can be crushed in seconds by torrents of water and mud that generate exceptional velocity and speed.

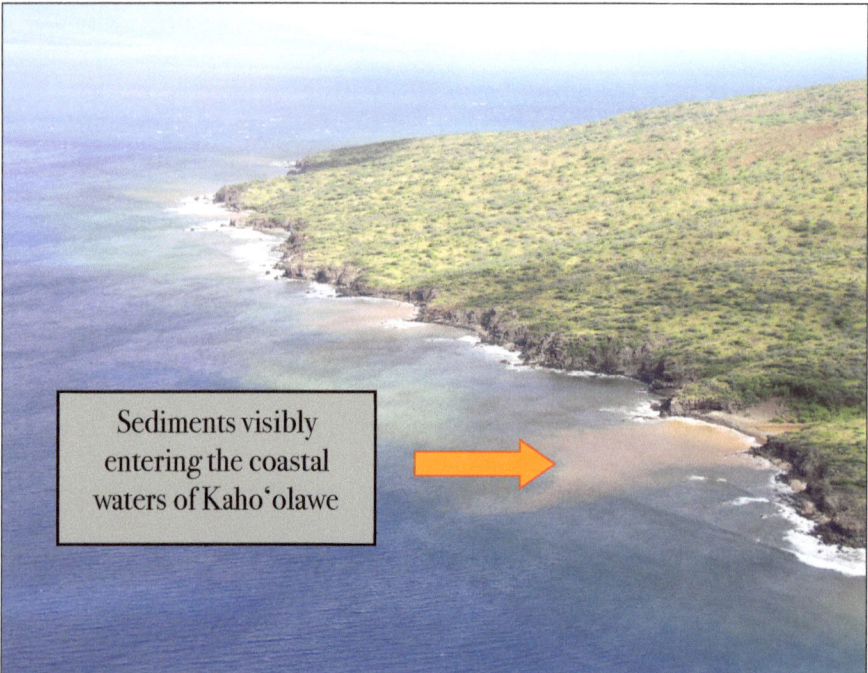

Sediments visibly entering the coastal waters of Kahoʻolawe

Sediment cloud offshore – Kahoʻolawe, Hawaiʻi.

Restoration work on Kahoʻolawe involving surface installation of Pili Bales to provide a micro-climate for plantings on the island.

Use of Pili/Coconut/or Plastic Rolls to act as sediment traps
on Kahoʻolawe.

The effectiveness of a sediment trap that is a part of restoration efforts on Kahoʻolawe.

The project that I designed was the largest non-military scientific research grant for the island at $2.5 million and envisioned determining if the volunteer restoration activities (hay bales, erosion control mats and other re-vegetation efforts) could impact the following: deter the erosion of the island, successfully re-establish it and measure the exact volume of sediment contained (if any) via the erosion control efforts.

Matthew L. Myers featured 3rd person from far right (in white) outlining strategy for the project.

Matthew L. Myers (center) featured with EPA and DOH officials at the
Navy landing point.

But the funding sought to measure something with more
far-reaching implications: Can densely populated communities
on the U.S. mainland and throughout the world design
infrastructure and erosion control systems to prevent and deter
storm events and flooding from ruining residential and
commercial properties costing insurance companies,
government and taxpayers billions of dollars in losses? This is a
problem worth tackling and investing in. It highlights the

critical nature of investing in research and development; and forming essential public and private partnerships.

The collapse of California Highway 101 in 2017 in Big Sur shut down the section of road feature (following page).

The road along Big Sur, California was completely shutoff when the entire portion of Highway 101 was covered with mudslide debris.

This caused the Big Sur community to be shut off from regular motor vehicle traffic. The impact to hotels, restaurants and business in the area was immediate: a precipitous loss in revenue.

Including a minor government surcharge, tolls and taxes for the region to finance similar research projects is necessary to model soil conditions and stability in the region, followed by installing erosion control systems that actually have the ability to contain tonnage of suspended sediments from runoff events. The long-term benefits of pro-active planning exceed the costs of a marginal tax in comparison to a catastrophic event, which causes millions of dollars of damage and auxiliary damage in a matter of hours.

The California Big Sur event could have been prevented (in part) by a comprehensive study acting in partnership with state, federal and local agencies, utilizing geological data and advanced erosion control methods, potentially saving the State of California millions of dollars in infrastructure repairs and tourism losses from an entire area becoming incapacitated by a hillside collapse.

The mudslides in Montecito, California, that occurred in 2017 after a nearly 300,000-acre fire followed by flash flooding were more devastating. They resulted in the loss of human lives, the disruption of a community and the loss of homes and businesses.

The collapse of the Oroville Dam spillway in California provides another example of how this research and restoration can be applied. Tens of thousands of residents were displaced by the physical failure of the spillway. The photos (on the following page) are from the Folsom Dam and its spillway. They illustrate the complexity of this engineering feat.

This is something that the research at Kahoʻolawe could have prevented. Extrapolating the expected and unexpected outcomes of this work, tailoring the monitoring for California conditions and then applying the results to earth works that directly control and contain soil destruction is imperative.

Folsom Dam, California includes a spillway and associated infrastructure that is similar to the Oroville Dam.

Spillway (center) at the Folsom Dam that is located approximately 70 miles from Oroville Dam.

The 247 acres Kahoʻolawe island restoration proposal involved installing USGS certified erosion pin transects, stream gauges and turbidity monitors to model soil loss, suspended sediment (stream gauges in Hakioawa and Kaulana transects;) and water turbidity (underwater tripod monitors also in Hakioawa and Kaulana bays) from extreme storm event conditions.

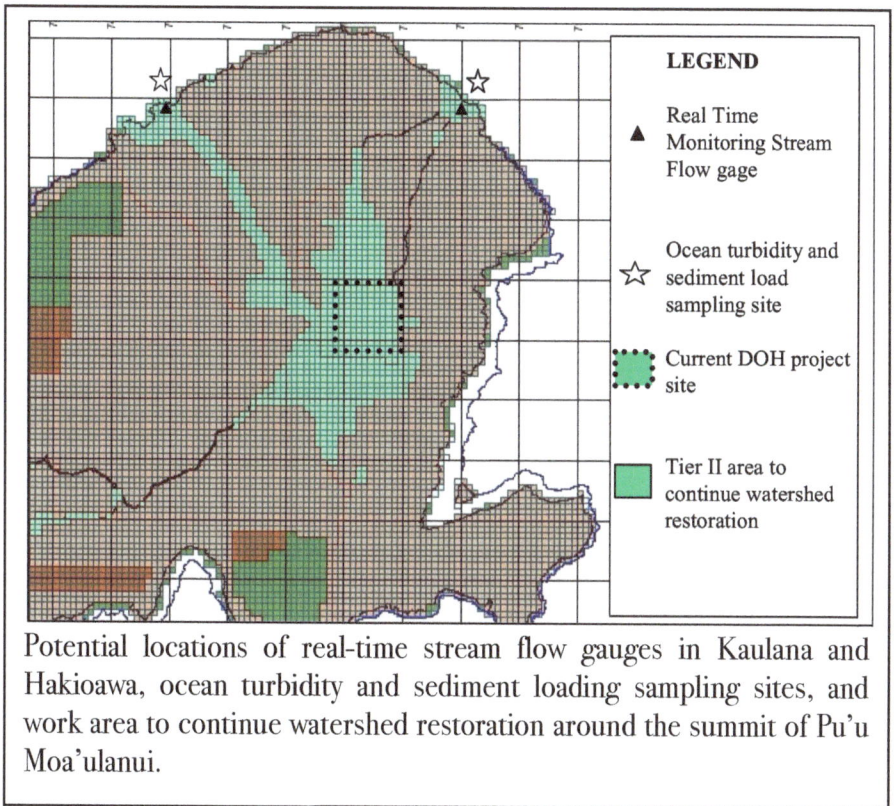

Potential locations of real-time stream flow gauges in Kaulana and Hakioawa, ocean turbidity and sediment loading sampling sites, and work area to continue watershed restoration around the summit of Pu'u Moa'ulanui.

The black square was the current area of restoration. The project expanded this project significantly beyond the original area to 100 hectares (ha). Image source: KIRC.

The project site would be located in Tier II (an area defined by KIRC and the Navy clear of ordinance and safe for traversing) areas near the shoreline areas of Kaulana and Hakioawa, and also in Tier II areas (ordinance cleared and denoted in green) around the summit of Kaho'olawe on Pu'u

Moaʻulanui (shown above). The project was originally proposed to be approximately 100 hectares (ha) or 247 acres. This proposal targeted Kaulana and Hakioawa watersheds specifically. There were several other watersheds emanating from the summit of Puʻu Moaʻulanui that also profited from the restoration activities, including, but not limited to, Kuheia.

The plan involved installing erosion pin transects at the summit of two major canyons on the island, stream gauges at the approximate half-way point of the selected canyons and turbidity monitors at the pre-determined locations on the ocean floor to capture measurements on visible sunlight and suspended sediments during storm events and after.

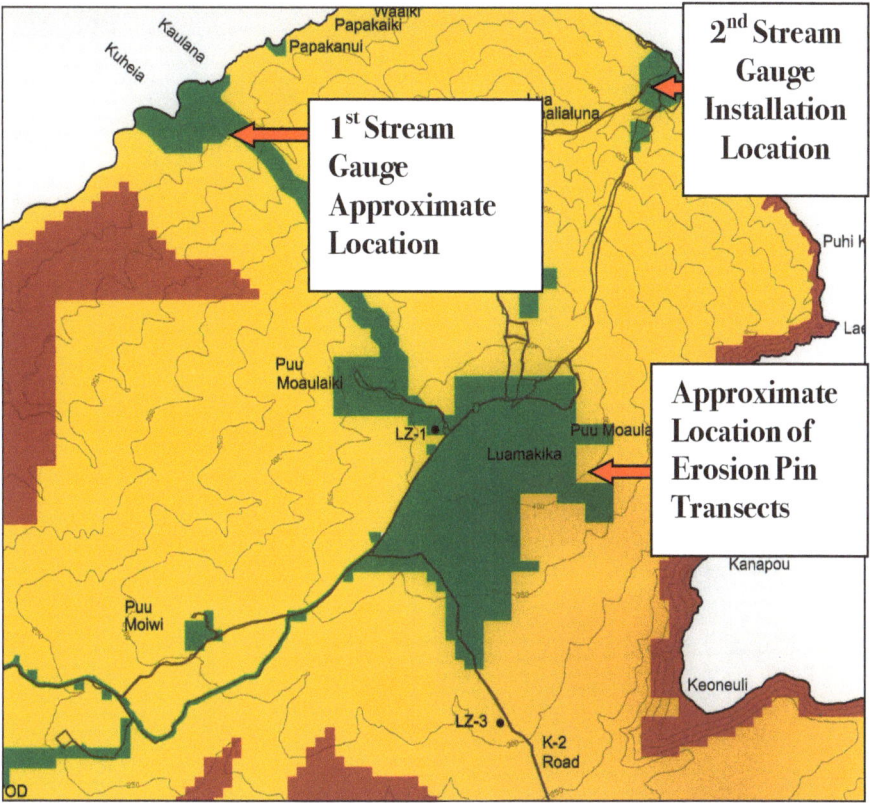

Map Showing Area of Proposed Monitoring Equipment Installation and Restoration Activities (Highlighted in Green). Red denotes areas filled with ordinances (unexploded and not safe to transverse).

Map showing original restoration site (square) and the additional 100 hectares of restoration work (two rectangle shaped overlays).

Digital Elevation Model (DEM) of Kahoʻolawe with current DOH Project Site and Kaulana and Hakioawa watersheds selected for restoration.

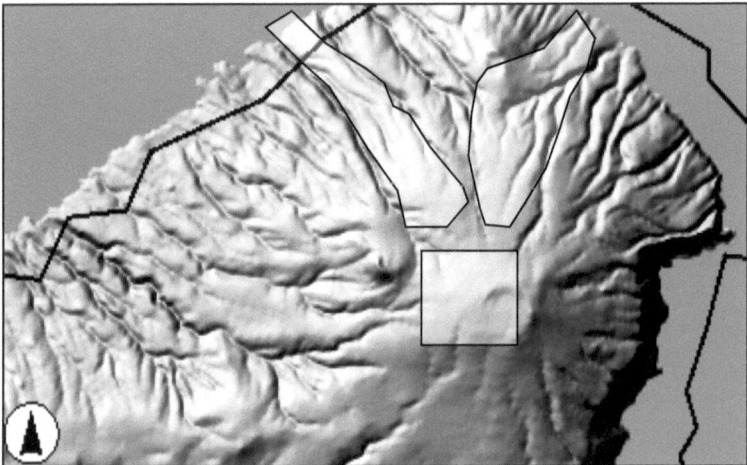

ELEVATION (CROSS SECTION) OF PROPOSED EROSION PIN TRANSECTS

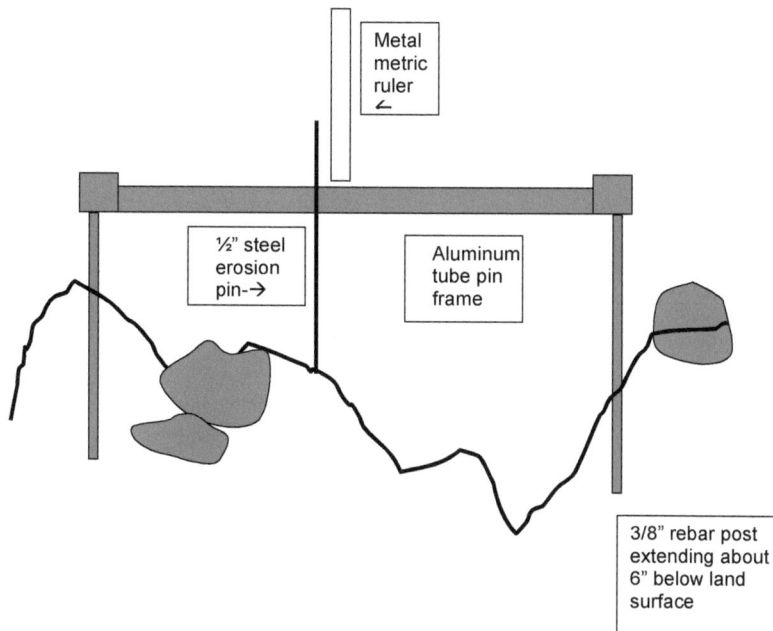

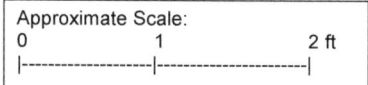

Metal metric ruler

½" steel erosion pin→

Aluminum tube pin frame

3/8" rebar post extending about 6" below land surface

Approximate Scale:
0   1   2 ft
|-------------------|--------------------|

ELEVATION (CROSS SECTION) OF PROPOSED STREAMGAGE (view downstream)

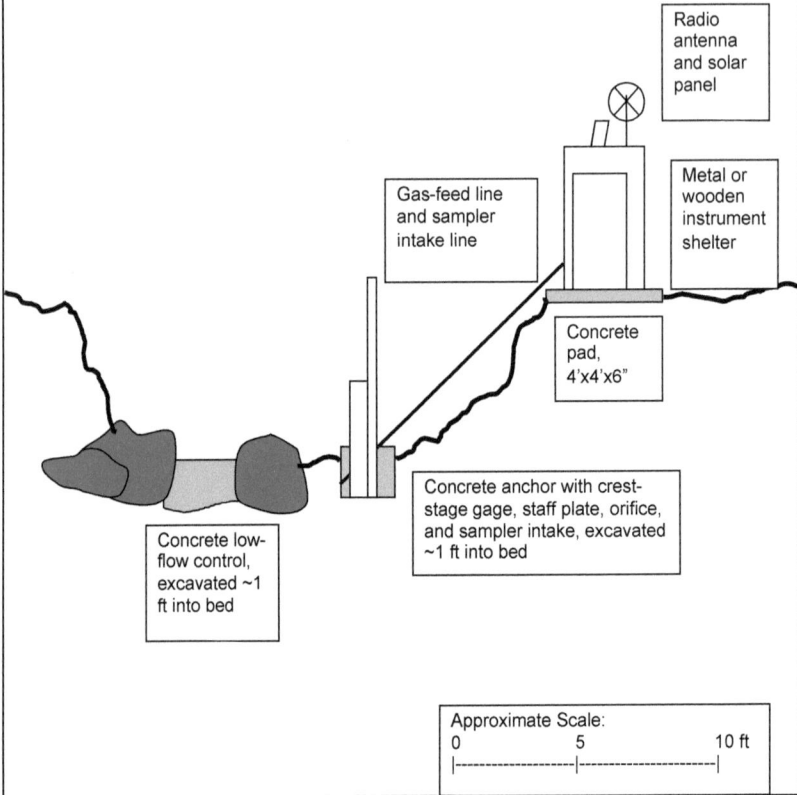

Radio antenna and solar panel

Gas-feed line and sampler intake line

Metal or wooden instrument shelter

Concrete pad, 4'x4'x6"

Concrete anchor with crest-stage gage, staff plate, orifice, and sampler intake, excavated ~1 ft into bed

Concrete low-flow control, excavated ~1 ft into bed

Approximate Scale:
0   5   10 ft
|-------------------|------------------------|

Volunteer activities for students, not-for profits and other community-based agencies had been conducted on the island for years based on military funded cleanup activities of remaining test ordinance buried in the soil in various locations; and subsequently with the transfer of the island's ownership to the State of Hawai'i through the Kaho'olawe Island Reserve Commission (KIRC).

Hay bays (and other indigenous plants) being delivered onto the summit of Kaho'olawe for restoration.

Hay bales and other materials were brought on-site from Molokai ranch and other locations.

Severe erosion on the island of Kahoʻolawe slopes.

Rain off the coast of Kahoʻolawe is visible in the distance. Hay bales and Pili rolls were used to control heavy erosion loss.

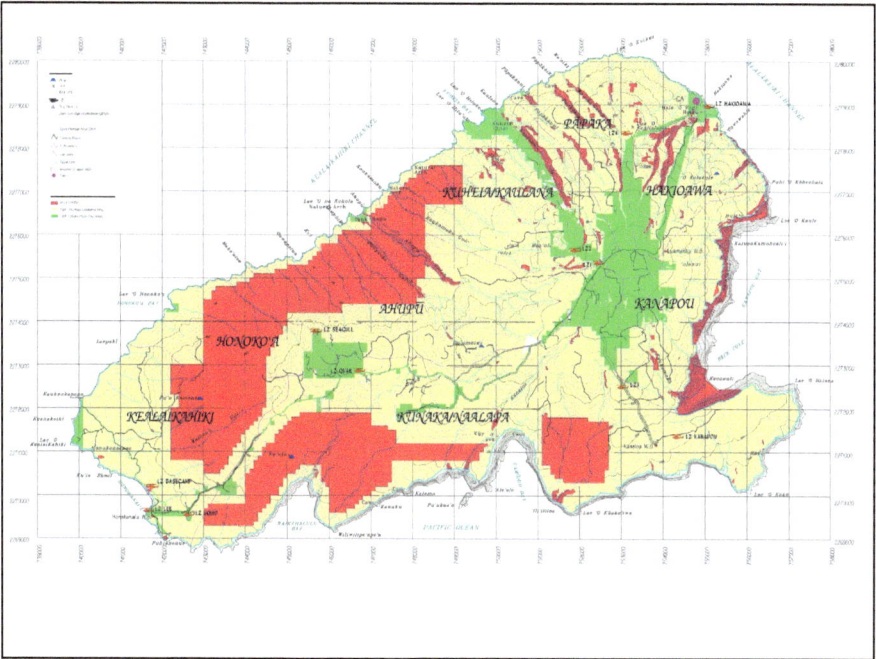

Map showing areas not cleared of ordinance (red) and restoration areas (green) on Kahoʻolawe. Image source: KIRC.

The map above shows the areas of new restoration in green. These are safe for volunteer activity. The areas denoted in red have ordinances (heavy explosives – mega ton) and are not accessible under any circumstances.

Map showing areas of pronounced hardpan (green) and
significant vegetation (purple to maroon) on Kahoʻolawe.

The map above shows the areas with the most pronounced
hardpan (nearly impenetrable soil). They are denoted in green.
Purple to maroon denotes areas of vegetation and new
restoration.

Satellite imagery showing areas of pronounced hardpan (brown) and significant vegetation (green) on Kahoʻolawe. Image source: KIRC.

The brown areas still require vegetation. As a consequence, they were the areas selected for restoration. The image on the following page denotes areas gridded out for restoration activities.

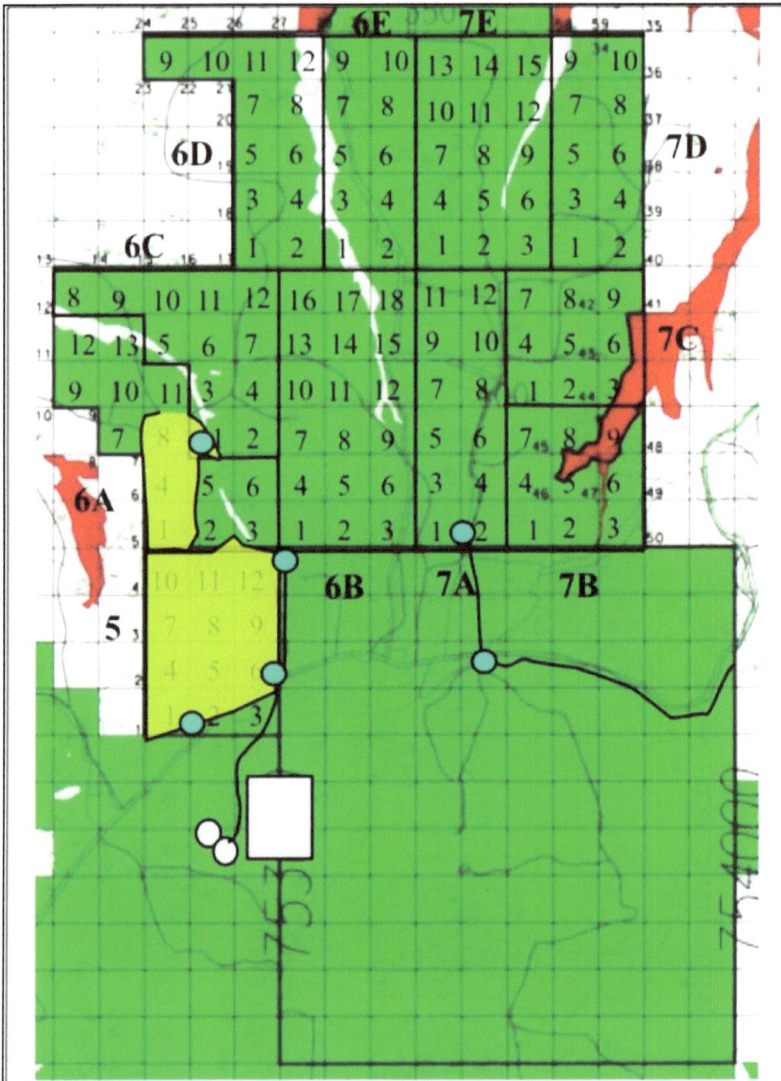

KIRC restoration sites denoted with specific numbers for tracking.

Volunteer ingenious planting restoration work being completed on island.

Volunteers planting indigenous trees from Maui nurseries brought to the island via barge and helicopter.

Matthew L. Myers (top right panel - center) and other members of the KIRC team removing turbidity monitors for calibration and data downloading diving 25 feet to the ocean floor.

The KIRC team accomplished free-diving 25 + feet to the ocean floor in heavy currents in Kahoʻolawe tiger-shark infested water (above). The location had been pre-screened for ordinance, but *only* in the locations where the tripods were installed. Under no circumstances should unauthorized personnel or recreational divers swim in these waters without clearance from the Navy, KIRC and/or written County of Maui or State of Hawaiʻi approval. There is a high level of risk for unexploded landmines that were not captured by the ordinance team that missed the island as a target originally and/or washed off the surface of the island during a storm.

Volunteers unloading hay bales onto the summit of Kahoʻolawe.

The project had a favorable outcome with measureable results, including both expected and unexpected variables. The photos on the following pages illustrate the success of the technical physical installations.

Included is the completed USGS stream gauge at the Kaulana watershed.

The stream gauges, turbidity monitors and erosion pin transects were connected with great succinctness.

Turbidity monitors on surface of Hakioawa and Kaulana bays. Divers scanning for ordinances on the surface of the ocean flow to avoid detonation.

What about the physical results? Did the restoration efforts control the erosion effectively? On an island-wide basis the answer is not conclusive. During winter months the Hakioawa watershed generates six times more sediment[3] than the Kaulana watershed. The EPA funded research expected more conclusive results. The EPA underwriting required specific measurable outcomes regarding sediment containment

---

[3]KIRC and USGS stream gauge data. 2006 to 2010.

based on the re-establishment activities. The 26 rebuilding sites when compared with the 51 non-restoration benchmark sites[4] showed no sediment loss (net zero) and some deposition of soil. However, these are small-localized site-specific successes when compared with the overall net loss of suspended sediment, which in 2008 and 2009 measured a collective total of 3,770 tons[5].

---

[4]*Id.*
[5]*Id.*

A Model for Improving Profitability for Banks and Insurance Companies

How can this type of equipment and data collection be tied to increasing the profitability of insurance companies, actuaries and banks? If the data generated from the equipment research equipment demonstrated that one valley was losing more sediment than another (using the Kahoʻolawe sites as an example), then restoration activities on the island could focus on the area with the greatest volume of sediment loss.

California and the western states are subject to fire and flash floods causing catastrophic damage in a matter of hours or days. The coastal areas throughout the Continental U.S., Alaska and Hawaiʻi are subject to hurricanes and tsunamis and storms have caused billions of dollars in damage. For the California mudslides and fires and the Louisiana and Texas hurricanes research combined with monitoring equipment that provided expected and unexpected outcomes could save banks and insurance companies billions of dollars. If they know that one watershed is more prone to erosion and flash floods during storm events then they can begin installing control equipment in those valleys, slopes and watersheds proactively, but only if they have installed the equipment in advance and studied the outcomes.

For example, planning for erosion control on the upslope area above a commercial development or site prevents future site damage. Designing barriers that combine permeable and impermeable materials can be implemented well in advance if building on a vacant lot, repurposing an abandoned shopping mall or redeveloping existing structures. Investing in sophisticated erosion controls upfront results in reduced insurance costs and a reduction in overall site damages later. Insurance companies benefit from lower premiums and small disaster payouts, improving the bottom line for shareholders and community-benefits for stakeholders. Downstream impacts to fisheries, factories, farms and other corporate entities that do not have to filter their water supply to ensure continued production.

Kahoʻolawe Net Results

The Kahoʻolawe project cost approximately $2.5 million. The losses from the storm events in California, Louisiana and Texas reached multi-billions. From a cost benefit analysis the benefits from a small investment in a project like Kahoʻolawe are exceptional. In California a couple of houses add up to several million dollars. Preventing a small community from washing away would quickly pay for itself. Most importantly in densely populated areas lives and businesses could be saved.

In the end thousands of volunteers were educated on geological restoration activities, including students and adults of all ages.

Kahoʻolawe volunteers preparing to head out into the field for a day of activity.

Kahoʻolawe is truly a magical place. Despite the heavy bombings several exceptional archaeological features remain including *the navigator's chair*. This was a stone seat that early Polynesians used to develop a complex navigation system for sailing throughout the Pacific based on observing the stars, wind patterns and currents, with a spectacular view of the surrounding Hawaiʻian islands.

The extraordinary Navigator's chair – a stunning Hawai'ian site.

Despite the heavy erosion the undisturbed ocean area surrounding the island (due to closure for explosives) is thriving with fish and marine life. Hawaiian spinner dolphins are visible in close proximity to the Navy base camp in the photo in the next page. I remember looking at the shore from the open gazebo having realized a dream that I had years ago in New York: that one day I would swim in close proximity with dolphins. At the time I was envisioning a warm tropical location, not necessarily the literal manifestation of this.

I never realized when I mentioned this to a colleague a Cornell that many years later I would find myself wading out into the ocean during the islands' volunteer swim break and doing exactly this.

Hawai'ian spinner dolphins crusin' on the Kaho'olawe shoreline.

Benefits of Implementing Erosion Control in High Risk Areas

It is essential for modern corporations to design their programs and projects with sustainability in mind. It is not a cursory expense. However, do projects generate enough business value to warrant the risks? Do the benefits outweigh the risks and costs of implementing these controls?

The answer is unequivocal: Yes.

The costs of failing to act quickly reach hundreds of millions or billions. The key is to mitigate the risk by implementing safety measures and wearing the proper safety equipment. Small safety measures can save lives and cost minimal dollar amounts. Teaching helicopter passengers how to cut their harnesses if they crash over water and are submerged is essential. Making sure participants wear goggles, safety glasses, ear protection and suits (chemical, fire, HAZMAT, et. al.),

The site below is located in a mountainous region with 70 to 100 mile-per-hour gusts and only accessed by experienced pilots with training in multiple theatres. The team wore flight suits, ear protection, communication helmets, boots (OSHA approved with steel toes) and safety equipment.

Heavy winds required that the pilot, co-pilot and passengers be securely fastened to their seats. All participants understood the risks and had signed liability waivers, in addition to receiving training on being submerged under water (and escape methods); and a review of crash landing safety over terrain.

Under no circumstances should recreational tourists venture into these types of areas without proper training and an experienced team.

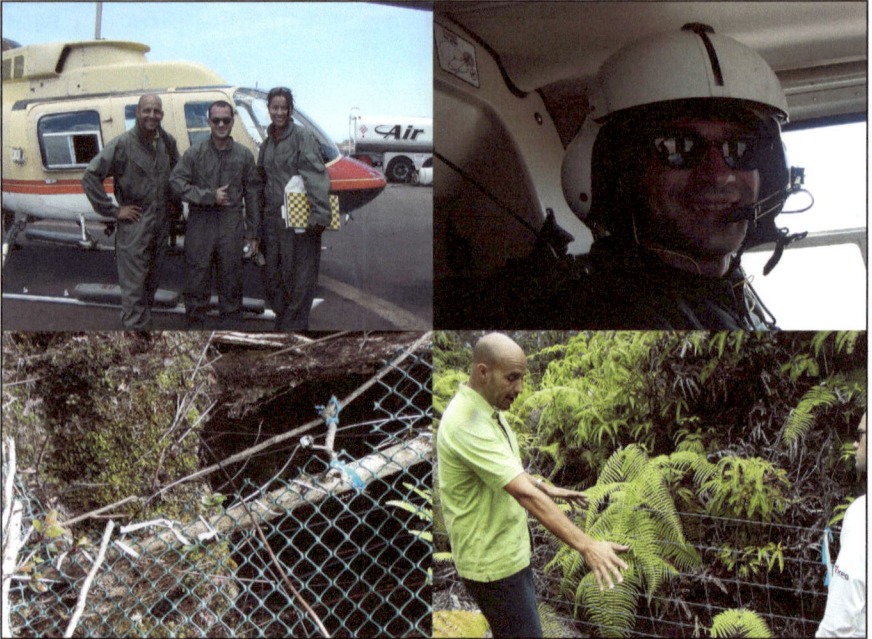

Team remote erosion control installation on undisclosed location.

The landing area, in this case required an exceptional pilot, experienced in landing under extremely challenging circumstances on a 25 square foot landing pad next to a sheer cliff with high risk of wind whiplash. There is a highly amplified and elevated risk of crashing into the mountainside. Heavy fumes enter the helicopter and can make the occupants sick. Passengers with heart conditions or other respiratory issues should avoid travel like this.

The project above illustrates how excellent erosion control starts in the mountains and continues down to coastal regions, creating a comprehensive and holistic approach to erosion control and proactive business development. However, it is only a valuable exercise if safety is integrated from the onset. In essence, earth-controls add value regardless of the difficulty of the terrain.

This is the future of planning and should be implemented by municipalities, governments and corporations whenever possible, but only if security measures are built into the process from the onset.

Designing Profitable Projects that Successfully Integrate Archaeology and Historic Sites

One of the constant conflicts that emerge in designing a large-scale development is historic preservation and archaeological sites. What happens when most of these items are located? They are photographed. A record is created. Then the sites are destroyed. It doesn't have to be resolved this way.

Why is this the case?

In most instances it is possible to integrate the needs of a business development with preservation of a spectacular archaeological site or areas of unique significance. It simply requires making minor changes to project design, which typically result in minimal expense.

Hiluhilu Development, LLC. Project Background

Hiluhilu Develop LLC. was a Limited Liability Corporation formed by the investor Charles Schwab in partnership with the University of Hawaiʻi. The site was envisioned to be a private and public partnership, with a portion of development completed by Hiluhilu Develop LLC and portion by the University of Hawaiʻi. Specifically the Palamanui Project by Hiluhilu Development, LLC. c/o Island Advisors, Inc. was designed to support the University of Hawaiʻi's proposed West Hawai'i campus located on a vacant 725.2 acre parcel in the North Kona Judicial District, Island of Hawai'i, Ahupua'a of Kau, TMK: (3)-7-2-05:01.

In examining the location through a review of the files, proposed blueprint maps and direct site visits it became clear that there were several unresolved issues with archaeological preservation and water usage that could be rectified with relatively simple project changes and minor blue print adjustments.

Sites of Significance Scheduled for Demolition

The archaeological sites that were scheduled for demolition are as follows: State Inventory of Historic Places (SIHP) Site 14375 (Features A-F) which include an integrated cave/lava tube, with associated *pamanū* for the *konane* game and a trail system. This combined group of features that was located at SIHP Site 14375[6] had more significance than the project archaeologists originally identified in their report.

The *pamanū* are identified in the report. However, an in-depth discussion was not provided regarding their cultural significance for early pre-contact Hawaiʻians.

---

[6]OHA staff has included *Figure 137. SIHP Site 14375 plan view* for further clarification on how these features are grouped together. Appendix C, Archaeological Inventory Survey, Volume 2: Appendices A-F, Final EIS for Hiluhilu Development, LLC. (A Charles Schwab project).

Preserving these features, the caves, the trail and associated *papamū*, was important because they appeared to have been a part of this intricate and complicated tax-collection and associated ceremony between the districts of Kau and Puna.[7]

These features were primarily destroyed, despite few (or no examples) at the State of Hawai'i's pre-eminent Bishop Museum, which houses Polynesian and Hawai'ian artifacts. They could have been transferred by barge and set up on the grounds of the Bishop Museum for other people to enjoy and learn about this complex and sophisticated culture that existed in pre-western contact.

---

[7]Excerpts from David Malo's 1951 text *Hawaiian Antiquities* are as follows: *Konane* tournaments may have been a minor feature of the *makahiki* games. *Hawaiian Petroglyphs* by J. Halley Cox and Edward Stasack in their 1970 Bishop Museum Special Publication, (Eighth printing 1999).

SIHP Site 14375 Photographs[8]:

SIHP Site 14375 (Feature C): Lava tube/cave habitation site.

These lava tubes were used for water collection and in some cases as burial sites and are not isolated features in the area.

---

[8]All photographs were taken by Matthew Myers, and were taken on an April 8, 2004 site visit to Hiluhilu Development, LLC.

SIHP Site 14375 (Feature D): Trail located near and around the caves and associated pamanū.

This trail was not a separate and distinct entity. It was connected to the cave systems located around it and would have been utilized by pre-contact Hawaiians. These trails should have been maintained, preserved and interconnected as a part of a system because as David Malo's notes in his 1951 text *Hawaiian Antiquities* "At the time of the tax-collecting and at the *makahiki* games, the procession of the Lono god image made use of the upper coastal trail."[9] This information was not expressly identified in the Final EIS for the proposed project and as a consequence this feature appears to be more significant than previously noted.

---

[9]*Id.*

SIHP Site 14375 (Feature C): *Pamanū*.

The museum grade game-board and absolutely stunning archaeological example scheduled for demolition.

SIHP Site 14375 (Feature E): *Pamanū*.

This is another excellent example of *pamanū* at the project site. As noted previously the project archaeologists did not recommend preservation of this site. It is a part of a large cave system that includes games at more than one location and includes a trail in the immediate vicinity.

Figure 137. SIHP Site 14375 Plan View[10]

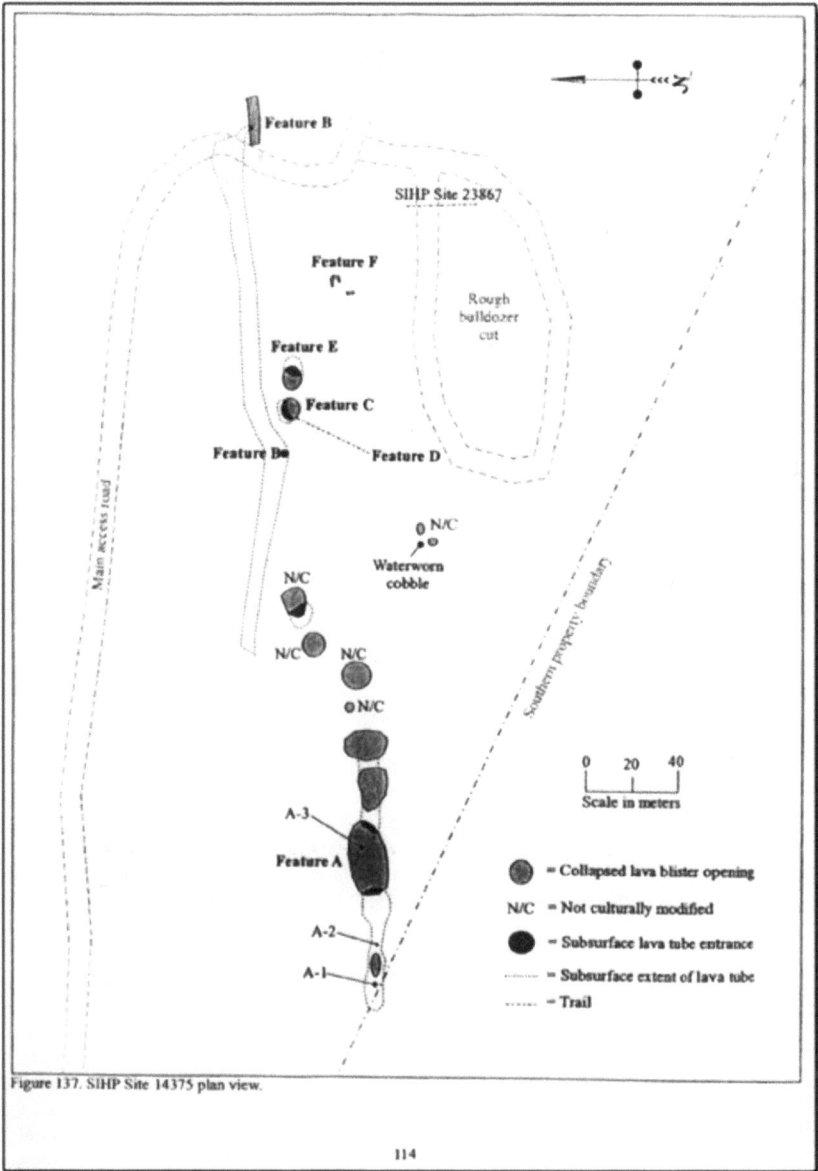

Figure 137. SIHP Site 14375 plan view.

114

---

[10]*Id.*, Refer to Footnote 2.

Feature C (on the diagram above) was an excellent example of a *pamanū* for the *konane* game. This game was not scheduled for preservation. The archaeological inventory survey recommends "No further work" for this site.[11]

---

[11]Noted in *The Significance Assessment and Treatment Recommendations*, Table 22. Site Significance and recommended treatments. (page 246). Appendix C, Archaeological Inventory Survey, Volume 2: Appendices A-F, Final EIS for Hiluhilu Development, LLC (owned in part by Charles Schwab the investor and banker).

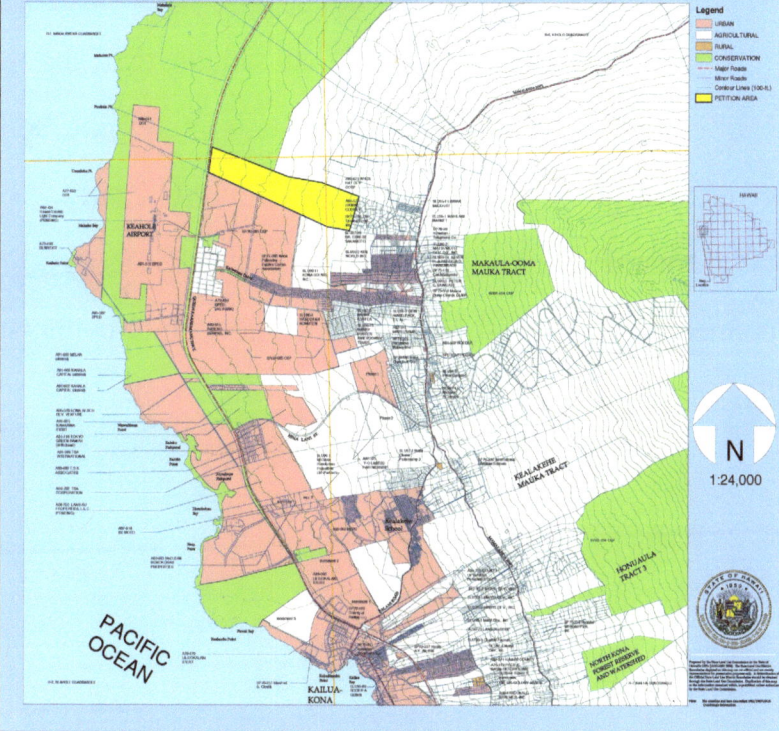

Image source: State of Hawai'i Land Use Commission.

It was also unclear why numerous other features located in the proposed project area were scheduled for demolition (data recovery, or no further work) rather than safeguarded, and why the trail system located in the schematic were not being preserved. The trail system included up to 15 SHIP sites.[12] On two occasions I requested that this trail system be recognized, and connected to established sites to create an interconnected system.

---

[12]It is unclear why these sites are not being scheduled for preservation.

Habitation Sites

The majority of the pre-contact temporary habitation complex (including platforms, terraces, enclosure, et. al., and agricultural features) was not scheduled for preservation by the archaeologists (or project developers). These features appeared to have been the living quarters and the associated agricultural production that supported the interconnected trail system along the upper coastal region in Kaū, for the tax-collection, associated *makahiki* festival/ceremonial activities, and procession of the Lono god image. These SIHP habitation sites were identified as follows: 14339, 14341-14345, 14346, 14347, 14350, 14351, 14354, 14365-14368, 14371-14373, 14374, 14375, 23862, 23864, 23866, 23867, 23870, 23876, 23880, 23881, 23885-23907.

I have never seen anything of the majesty and caliber of this archaeology in the collections of the British Museum, The American Museum of Natural History; or even the Bishop Museum, which is located on O'ahu, Hawai'i. It is a tragedy that no compromise could be made on the part of the developers to create simple exclosures or even ship the artifacts to the Bishop Museum. As a consequence of the archaeological significance of the area, I recommended that a larger percentage of these sites be preserved in place.

Stunning on-site archaeological site.

Regarding this case the developers sent agents to my family's home to photograph them – my father who is from Chicago and New York ran outside and attempted to chase them in our car. A personal conversation was conducted with the director of the agency the day after, noting that this was absolutely unacceptable. However, this is a typical form of harassment and intimidation that developers use to prevent opposition to their projects.

What the developers failed to understand was the nuanced nature and intent of the original request: provide a simple barrier (i.e. wooden posts with rope and simple signage) around the majestic Konane game board and Ali'i chief cave and trail system.

Business developments can proceed that integrate cultural and archaeological features. This particular project was delayed several years, but ultimately the majority of the archaeological sites were demolished. Particularly troublesome was the disregard for Hawai'ian culture, despite the heavy marketing of a Hawai'ian "state of place" and indigenous culture by the State of Hawai'i and developers for tourism.

Konane Game Board of the Aliʻi chiefs of old.

As an active golfer I was never opposed to the development or a golf course, only to the 100% total bulldozing of this splendid location, which could have easily been solved with a simple and inexpensive post-roped fences; (or as previously noted shipping the features to the Bishop Museum on Oʻahu) – allowing the golf game to continue undeterred.

Matthew L. Myers (front second to right) organizer of the 1st of a series of golf tournaments for his EMBA University of Hawai'i at Manoa classmates, clearance for this military course provided by Hawai'i's Air Force General (1st to right- rear).

Matthew L. Myers (center - rear) organizer of the 2nd of a series of golf tournaments for his EMBA University of Hawai'i at Manoa classmates, clearance for this military course provided by Hawai'i's Air Force General (front - center).

Hiluhilu Development, LLC Water Supply Issues

One of the concerns for the Hiluhilu Development, LLC project was the issue of fresh water for the site. As a consequence, I requested a review of water supply availability/requirements by the Department of Water Supply, County of Hawaii regarding the Final Environmental Impact Statement (EIS) for the Proposed Palamanui Project by Hiluhilu Development, LLC. c/o Island Advisors, Inc. The Final EIS was prepared as a part of the process for the project developer's (Hiluhilu Development, LLC) December 2003 petition to the State Land Use Commission (LUC) for reclassification of Conservation and Agricultural lands to Urban (260.7 acres are in the Conservation District, 464.5 acres are in the Agriculture District) by the State Land Use Commission.

I had several concerns regarding the availability of a sufficient sustainable source of groundwater to meet the demands of the project developers. It is an excellent example of where compromise should occur. Business needs can be met in tandem with archaeology, water, natural resource and other issues. It is *never* necessary for 100% demolition and/or clear-cutting of an entire forest (as an example). There is always a means of maintaining high profitability and balancing multiple shareholder interests.

This project is reviewed because ensuring safe and clean drinking water is essential to any large-scale development. A project of this size that also includes a golf course can benefit from the use of grey water to irrigate the grounds, particularly on the arid and dry Kona coast from mauka to makai.

Water Supply Issues

A request was made for additional review and clarification of the groundwater availability (recharge rates) from the U.S. Geological Survey, Hawaii District Office and Clark C. K. Liu, Civil Engineering at the University of Hawaii at Manoa (with expertise on hydrology issues). I asked that these entities review Appendix J: "Groundwater Resources of Kau, North Kona, Hawaii: A Water Study for Hiluhilu Development, LLC" in relationship to the project developers Palamanui project requirements outlined in Chapter 3.0, Project Description (3.2.7.4 Water System and 3.2.7.5 Wastewater System) and the overall project for the Re-Submitted Final Environmental Impact Statement for the Proposed Palamanui Project by Hiluhilu Development, LLC., located at TMK: (3)-7-2-05:01.

In addition my previous letters to the State LUC and Group 70 International, Inc., the March 2004 Draft Report Ka'u to South Kona Water Master Plan (prepared for the County of Hawai'i's Office of the Mayor) provides additional documentation of water supply issues that the North Kona area faces. The report notes the following points of significance: "Generally, fresh water is identified above the 2,000 foot elevation. Areas below this elevation are not suitable for potable well development."[13] If the project developers are forced to rely on wells drilled for potable water below the 2,000-foot elevation, it was unclear that the proposed area will be able to meet Hiluhilu Development LLC's outlined project requirements for water. Additionally, my April 7, 2004 letter to the LUC noted:

---

[13]Chapter I, Page 9. Draft Report Ka'u to South Kona Water Master Plan. March 2004.

"Currently, it appears that the project will require 2,206,000 gpd (potable and non-potable) water sources and that Hiluhilu Development, LLC has guaranteed access to only 205,800 gpd (potable water) through their Department of Water Supply agreement, leaving them to find sources for 2,000,200 gpd.[14] Two uncompleted wells (potable water) located on the north and south corners of the Mākālei Estates have a potential production capacity of 750,000 gpd, totaling 1,500,000 gpd. If they are completed they would cover the requirements for potable water sources. However, it is unclear when these wells will be completed, leaving a deficit in the interim. Additionally, it is unclear if the 3 private non-potable brackish wells proposed to cover the 1,000,000 gpd requirement to irrigate the golf course, in the 10 year interim for the scheduled completion of the proposed 850,000 gpd wastewater treatment plant."

The April 2004 Re-Submitted Final EIS indicates,

---

[14]Portions of this paragraph are included in the Department's April 7, 2004 letter to the project consultants, Group 70 International, Inc.

"The proposed water distribution system will extend the existing 12-inch water main in Mākālei Estates down to the village center area and provide a connection to the UH West Hawai'i Campus parcel at the village center location. It will also make possible connection to the County water main in Queen Ka'ahumanu Highway at the Kona International Airport access road via the two 0.5 million gallon (MG) reservoirs at the 280-foot elevation mauka of the airport access road. This connection is desirable to the Department of Water Supply so that they can move water from supply wells in the mauka areas to satisfy demands along Queen Ka'ahumanu Highway north of Kailua-Kona."

It was ambiguous from the reports originally commissioned by the developers that the Department of Water Supply, County of Hawaii would actually be able to support the water requirement needs for the proposed project, if the private wells (3 brackish wells) and the uncompleted Kau Wells 1 and 2 fail to produce the water necessary to accommodate the plan.

I requested that the Environmental Impact Statement (EIS) for the project be revised to provide the public with the following clarifications:

It is also not clear whether or not the area's groundwater supply would yield the projected amounts of water from the 3 brackish (for non-potable water) wells and the 2 additional (potable water) wells proposed to be drilled on the property. The U.S. Geological Survey, Hawaii District Office has indicated that it should have the opportunity to comment and review on this project, particularly the "Groundwater Resource of Kau, North Kona, Hawaii" prepared by Waimea Water Services, because of their expertise on the area (groundwater recharge rates and groundwater supply in the project area). The public and the constitutionally protected competing interests for water in the area are legally entitled to a categorically complete EIS which provides additional documentation and review of available groundwater resources and recharge rates by Federal and State agencies. The EIS is not complete at this point. The LUC, in accordance with Chapter 343, HRS, should not accept the project developers petition to reclassify the subject parcel's 725.2 acres to Urban District from Agriculture and Conservation until water supply requirements are identified, tested for and met. The disclosure of probable impacts from the proposed project is insufficient and the public is entitled to a document with more details regarding the adequacy of water supply on the proposed site (particularly if drawing upon the aquifer under the project site) will negatively impact businesses and residents in the area in the long term.

Additionally, Pursuant to Chapter 15-15-18, Hawaii Administrative Rules (HAR), Standards for determining "U" Urban district boundaries, (2), "(B) Availability of basic services such as schools, parks, wastewater systems, solid waste disposal, drainage, water, transportation systems, public utilities, and police and fire protection; and (C) Sufficient reserve areas for foreseeable urban growth," need to be considered prior to the LUC's reclassification of the subject parcel. The project doesn't have a legal guarantee to all of the water that it needs for the proposed project, and <u>Chapter 15-15-18, HAR is established to determine if sufficient water and wastewater systems will be present to support the project</u>. It is not clear that sufficient groundwater will be available to support the potential Urban District reclassification. Additionally, the Proposed Final EIS notes that the 850,000 gpd wastewater treatment plant will not be completed until the 10 build out is finalized. As a consequence, the land (TMK: (3)-7-2-05:01) should not be reclassified until the project developers can demonstrate that enough groundwater exists (and a sufficient wastewater system will be present) in the project area to support the golf course, residential and commercial and improvements over the long term (groundwater recharge rate) and that the potential project will not require an expensive County of Hawai'i water main, which area businesses and residents will finance (through the issuance of Bonds or otherwise) if the 5 private wells fail to yield their expected water return in the long term.[15]

Why is all of this so critical?

With periods of extreme weather, particularly droughts it is essential to determine if a project's water demands can be met by existing water tables. San Diego, California has responded to this issue by building a desalination plant, a smart strategic move for the future.

The issue of salinity inversion – where ocean water replaces fresh water as it is extracted for use is particularly acute in the Hawai'ian islands, due to the geological construction of the islands. Fresh water in Hawai'i is derived from a volcanic-rock aquifer, with fresh water being trapped in a lens (a transition area between brackish water and freshwater)[16].

If too much water (for a golf course, or commercial and/or recreational use) is extracted the water table collapses and is converted from fresh water into brackish water and finally salt water.

---

[15]Matthew L. Myers April 21, 2004 Letter to the State of Hawai'i Land Use Commission (LUC) on behalf of OHA.
[16]USGS Groundwater in Hawai'i. Fact Sheet. 2000.

This can have catastrophic results to the economic viability of community requiring emergency high interest bonds to finance a desalination plant at extraordinary cost to the community at large.

The Complexities of Securing Revenues for Native Americans and Tribes

Securing revenue from Native American treaties is a very specialized and specific endeavor. Attached is my summary of issues regarding ceded lands inventories. It is included because businesses with mining and other natural resource extraction-based companies often struggle with the complexity of land rights. The same is true in the U.S. West where water rights are grandfathered into many land use agreements. In California, for example, most of the large-scale farming operations have water rights that pre-empt new users (i.e. new commercial residential and commercial developments). As a consequence, entering into a contact to ensure that all parties are made financially whole is essential.

Ceded Lands Inventories Background

The Office of Hawaiian Affairs (OHA) appeared to be in possession of three principle inventories[17] of ceded lands (encumbrances and general listings). Additional updates have also been distributed to OHA by DLNR (DLNR Receivable Aging as of 02/29/2004 and 03/312004 with an accounting of term easements, fiscal deposits, leases (ocean), leases (land), permits (land), et. al.).

---

[17]One of the inventories is a physical copy from DLNR dated 09/28/98 and the other copies are electronic Excel documents, SLIMS Inventory and SLIMS Encumbrance dated 10/25/2003.

09/28/98 Department of Land and Natural Resources (DLNR) List

A State of Hawaii, Department of Land and Natural Resources (DLNR), Land Management Division, Report No. CEBC1C1R, Run Date: 09/28/98 was prepared which included the following information: Tax Map Key (TMK), Encumbrance type, Document number, Name of user, Land area, District, Title Stat (**A**=State lands acquired under Section 5A of the Admissions Act, Public law 86-3, **B**=State lands acquired under 5E of the Admissions Act, **E**=State lands acquired under 5E of the Admission Act, **I**=Submerged lands referred to under Section 5I of the Admission Act, **X**=State lands acquired after Statehood. August 21, 1959, **Y**=State lands acquired through Federal Fee Surplus Property, Public Benefit Discount.

Federal Property and Administrative Services Act of 1949. (63 Stat 377) and the Surplus Property Act of 1944 (58 Stat 765), and Z=State lands acquired under Public Law 88-2333 77 Stat 472[18]

---

[18]These title codes were clarified for OHA on 12/7/93 by DLNR staff member Stephen Fan. However, the run date, as noted above for the particular inventory that OHA staff has been reviewing is 09/28/98. Presumably an inventory from 1993 from DLNR also exists (or was created at some point).

10/25/2003 SLIMS Inventory

On 10/25/2003 an electronic inventory was prepared by DLNR with the following owner information (State of Hawaii, State-DLNR, State-UH, State-HCDA[19], State-HCDCH[20]).

It is important to note that some of the lands under DLNR's jurisdiction are also associated with the Department of Hawaiian Homelands (DHHL). Trust Land Status (TLS) is listed in accordance with Public Law (PL) 86-3 (the Admission Act, Section 5). Additionally, the following qualifications are made in the database:

- Acquired after 8/59

---

[19]Acronym is for the Hawaii Community Development Association, which has the following purpose: "The Hawaii Community Development Authority's (HCDA) mission is to ensure that the Kakaako District is invigorated and established as a dynamic urban neighborhood, one which will accommodate a mix of people with a wide spectrum of activities and commerce. The HCDA was created by the 1976 State Legislature to bring about the timely planning, regulation and development of underutilized areas in the State. The strategically located, 670-acre Kakaako District was designated as the HCDA's first 'community development district'."

[20]Acronym is for the Housing and Community Development Association of Hawaii. This organization's mission per there website is as follows: "To serve as a catalyst to provide Hawaii's residents with affordable housing and shelter opportunities in a balanced and supportive environment without discrimination."

Lands acquired by the State through condemnation, conveyance in fee, etc.; does not include lands exchanged for 5(b), 5(e) or PL 88-233 lands -- there is a project underway to audit several hundred parcels with this coding to verify their status.

- PL 88-233

Lands that were held by the federal government under section 5(c) or 5(d) of PL 86-3, and conveyed to the State more than five years after statehood; and lands on Sand Island that the federal government held title to after 1963 and later declared surplus and conveyed to the State.

- **Fed Surplus**

Lands that the federal government acquired and later conveyed to the State.

- **Blank**

During the conversion from the mainframe, the Trust Land Status for some parcels was not transferred to SLIMS. In area, it is not a significant percentage of the State-owned lands, but it is significant in terms of numbers of parcels. There is a project underway by the abstracting section to make a determination for these parcels (priority is by size of the parcel). Finally, parcel area is defined in acreage.

10/25/03 SLIMS Encumbrance

On 10/25/2003 an electronic inventory was prepared by DLNR with the following information:

- ### Document Number

A unique alphanumeric identifier for the legal document for this encumbrance (e.g., gl1234, for General Lease number 1234; rp5678, for Revocable Permit number 5678; etc.).

- ### Name

The billing name for this account/encumbrance is also included.

- ### Status

Only current encumbrances (status = '0') are included in this listing.

- <u>Type</u>

Type of encumbrance is defined in the Excel database.

- <u>Character of Use</u>

A Brief descriptive categorization of the type of lease or permit is provided as a category in this SLIMS database.

- <u>Leased Area</u>

Total area in acres under this lease/permit.

In most cases this will match the parcel area. In some cases, the area under the lease/permit may be less than the parcel area (if the full parcel is not encumbered); or the leased area may be more than the parcel associated with it in this listing, if more than one parcel is encumbered– in that case, you'll see this lease/permit listed multiple times (with identical information), once for each of the encumbered parcels.

- <u>Unit</u>

A field in the property management database that is used to link the encumbrance with the Property code.

<u>Owner</u>

Information under the owner category is as follows:

  o Fee title holder (only certain state agencies may hold fee title to land);
  o For this download only parcels whose fee title holder is identified as 'State-DLNR' or the generic 'State of Hawaii' (i.e., no specific agency identified in SLIMS) are included -- other state agencies, federal and county agencies and private properties are explicitly excluded;
  o An exception is that some lands held in fee by the University of Hawai'i (UH) may be

included. If the instrument conveying the land from DLNR to UH is an Executive Order (EO), then the owner is shown as 'State-DLNR' or 'State of Hawaii' in this download.

Additional Updates

As noted previously, additional updates have also been prepared by the DLNR for OHA (DLNR Receivable Aging as of 02/29/2004 and 03/312004 with an accounting of term easements, fiscal deposits, leases (ocean), leases (land), permits (land), et. al.).

I originally was concerned with the following issues regarding the ceded land inventories that DLNR has prepared: It was unclear that the ceded lands inventories that DLNR has prepared for OHA (currently and in the past) are complete.[21] For example, if a percentage criterion[22] was used, it would not be a complete list of ceded lands. For example, see the table below:

DLNR Criteria for Including Lands in their Ceded Land Inventories	
Included in inventory:	*Not included in inventory*:
Greater than 50% of the subject parcel	Less than 50% of the subject parcel

Business Negotiation Outcomes

The ultimate outcome of this negotiation was the successful securement of nearly $10 million dollars in ceded

---

[21]This would include lands that DLNR leases, permits, et. al. (if applicable).

[22]A percentage criteria could include the following: including a parcel of land in a DLNR inventory based on a subject parcel having a percentage (%) great than x, or excluding a parcel of land if it had less than percentage (%) x.

land development that could be used for Native Hawai'ian development, housing and cultural preservation. This type of revenue is critical for preserving archaeological features like the Konane game boards (described extensively above), language and cultural practices of the Hawai'ian people.

Integrating Indigenous Culture Into The Business Framework For Funding

Many Federal, State and local programs integrate the surrounding communities into their funding streams, through request for proposals (RFPs), grants and other funding mechanisms.

Native Hawaiʻian activist and team at the site of Ke Kiaʻi a federal grant for indigenous plant stream bank restoration. Note: The 17 gauge rifle for rodents.

Mauka to Makai mural proudly being displayed as a part of the project.

So why is it so important to integrate the community into funding initiatives?

It's more than imperative -- it is essential for people to take ownership as stakeholders. One of the problems for community based organizations is they lack the resources or training to complete the reporting requirements, particularly accounting tied to specific deliverables. If these deliverables include erosion control or large-scale earth works with plantings they often do not have the equipment or the scale, like the USGS, to meet the demanding requirements of these programs.

The Complexities of Business Transactions with Native American Tribes

Treaties

From a business perspective there are unique distinctions between Native American tribes on the U.S. mainland and Hawaiʻi. These are based on treaties. Many of the U.S. tribes throughout the continental U.S. negotiated legal contracts in the form of treaties tied to land agreements with limited sovereignty. These complicate water rights, mining for natural resources or drilling for oil; and/or other business opportunities, including casinos.

In Hawaiʻi Native Hawaiʻians do not have a sovereign nation (or a land agreement) based on a specific treaty with the United States government. They receive limited subsidized housing and water rights from State of Hawaiʻi agencies, including the Department of Hawaiʻian Homelands (DHHL) that are limited to those people that can confirm that they are Native Hawaiʻian.

For example, Waimanalo, Oʻahu has multiple DHHL houses. However, DHHL housing doesn't confer sovereignty rights to their owners. In essence, DHHL housing confirms housing rights to families and individuals, but is based on an agreement between the State of Hawaiʻi and those individual families. However, those Native American families have *not* been granted the right by the State of Hawaiʻi to author a State Constitution, with there own rules and regulations. The same is true for the relationship between DHHL housing and the Federal government. Native Hawaiʻians are still bound by the rules and regulations of the Federal government. Many Native Hawaiʻians seek to create their own nation state. However, at this point in time they can't build roads, organize a police force or an army, negotiate agreements with foreign governments, or even set up a casino on DHHL lands.

Introduction on Sovereignty

The issue of Native American sovereignty historically has been a complex problem for the judicial, executive and legislative branches of the United States government. Once the courts defined sovereignty, the federal government faced the difficult task of designing policies and programs that respect tribal jurisdiction and self-sufficiency. The problem of Native American sovereignty has not been laid to rest by Supreme Court's rulings or the federal government's attempts to create programs and policies that provide a financial support network for tribes, while respecting their sovereignty. Federal environmental laws have particularly challenged Native American sovereignty. The principle question that this thesis will answer is: How is federal, state, and tribal jurisdiction affected by the implementation of federal environmental laws?

The question of whether Native American sovereignty affects the implementation of environmental law has been a widely misunderstood area of jurisdictional rights. Many Indian tribes control territory within a larger state and possess limited sovereignty from that state and the federal government. However, point and non-point source pollutants that might be discharged from tribal lands are not limited to the geographical area that they originate from, and as a result, federal environmental laws apply to tribal lands.

While tribal territories are subject to federal environmental laws, according to Charlotte Uram and Mary J. Decker in their article *Jurisdiction Over Water Quality on Native American lands*, two principal questions remain: "(1) to what extent can state or local governments implement and enforce federal, state or local environmental programs on tribal lands; and (2) what is the nature and scope of environmental protection programs that tribes may implement in Indian country."[23]

---

[23]Mary J. Decker and Charlotte Uram. "Jurisdiction Over Water Quality." *The Journal of Natural Resources & Environmental Law.* Journal of Natural Resources and Environmental Law. Vol. 8. No.1, 1992-1993.

The Supreme Court's Rulings on Tribal Sovereignty

The issue of whether or not Native American tribes or reservations are sovereign or "independent of all others [a *sovereign* state]"[24] historically has been an issue of contention for the United States. Article I, Section 2 of the United States Constitution indicates that Indians are not to be taxed and Article I, Section 8 indicates that Congress has the ability "To regulate commerce with foreign nations, and among the several states, and with the Indian tribes"[25].

Article VI of the Constitution holds that treaties that are backed by Congress to be the supreme law of the land.[26] The Constitution, however, is not explicit is in its definition of what constitutes Native American sovereignty.

---

[24]"Sovereign." *Third College Edition of American English: Webster's New World Dictionary.*

[25]U.S. Constitution, Article I, Section 2 and Section 8.

[26]Timothy Egan. "New Prosperity Brings New Conflict to Indian Country." Parallel Nations. First of Two Articles. *The New York Times.* March 8. 1998.

The vagueness of the Constitution has led to: (1) numerous Supreme Court cases that attempt to clarify the jurisdiction question in areas involving the Native American welfare state, environmental protection, and economic policy; and (2) the complex issue of how the federal government should allocate resources, programs and activities while respecting tribal sovereignty.

The U.S. Supreme Court and Native American Sovereignty

In 1831, the Supreme Court in the case *Cherokee Nation v. Georgia* ruled upon the problematic issue of Native American sovereignty. In *Cherokee Nation,* the State of Georgia was seeking to dissolve the Cherokee nation through legislative action.[27] The Cherokee nation filed a motion, under the Constitutional provision which gives the Supreme Court jurisdiction in disputes involving a State of the United States or the citizens thereof, and a foreign state, citizens, or subjects thereof are parties, seeking an injunction to restrain the State of Georgia from exercising their legislative power over an adjacent group of people asserting their independence. Chief Justice Marshall delivered the majority opinion of the Court. The fundamental question that Marshall raised was do the Cherokees constitute a foreign state in the sense of the Constitution?

---

[27]This paragraph is focused on *Cherokee Nation v. Georgia,* 30 U.S. 1 (1831), unless otherwise noted.

Though the Indians are acknowledged to have unquestionable, and heretofore unquestioned right to the lands they occupy, until that right shall be extinguished by a voluntary cession to our government, yet it may well be doubted whether those tribes that reside within the acknowledged boundaries of the United States can, with strict accuracy, be denominated foreign nations. They occupy a territory to which we assert a title independent of their will, which must take effect in point of possession when their right of possession ceases. Meanwhile they are in a state of pupilage. Their relation to the United States resembles that of a ward to his guardian.[28]

---

[28] *Id.*

Marshall held that although the argument for recognizing the Cherokee nation as a foreign state was compelling, the laws of our Government unquestionably recognize the Cherokee nation as a State, and the Courts are under legal obligation to abide by those acts. The Court ruled that because the Cherokee nation was not a foreign state in the sense of the Constitution it has does not have the authority to perpetuate litigation in the Courts of the United States. Marshall held that even though the Court might sympathize with the concerns of the Cherokee nation, restraining the State of Georgia was outside of the Court's jurisdiction and an injunction could not be issued on this basis.

The controversy of Native American sovereignty was not laid to rest in *Cherokee Nation v. Georgia.* In *Lone Wolf v. Hitchcock* the question of Native American jurisdiction emerged once again.[29] In *Lone Wolf,* a dispute emerged over the Congressional allotment of surplus acres of tribal grazing land to white settlers. The confederated tribes in *Lone Wolf* argued that Congress did not have the power to manage the property of Indians. Justice White delivered the majority opinion. The Court held that although the United States has recognized in legal contracts or treaties the Indian right of occupancy of tribal lands, the administration of tribal lands by Congress has never been disputed.

---

[29]This paragraph is focused on *Cherokee Nation v. Georgia,* 30 U.S. 1 (1831), unless otherwise noted.

The contention in effect ignores the status of the contracting Indians and the relation of dependency they bore and continue to bear towards the government of the United States. To uphold the claim would be to adjudge that the indirect operation of the treaty was to materially limit and qualify the controlling authority of Congress in respect to the care and protection of the Indians, and to deprive Congress, in a possible emergency, when the necessity might be urgent for a partition and disposal of tribal lands, of all power to act, if the assent of Indians could not be obtained.[30]

Justice White held that Congress had the power to dissolve a treaty between the United States and an Indian tribe. The Court ruled that because the Indians had not been released from the protection of the United States they are subject to legislative control by Congress.

---

[30] *Id.*

In 1959 the Supreme Court in *Williams v. Lee* again ruled upon Native American sovereignty.[31] In *Lee,* a non-Indian operating a store within the Navajo nation sued an Indian customer in the State of Arizona courts claiming that the customer had not paid for merchandise sold to him on credit. The Native American appealed to the Court arguing that State courts did not have jurisdiction in the case. The Supreme Court held that under treaties with the Navajo's, jurisdiction over the internal affairs rested with existing Tribal governments. The Court ruled that because the Navajo Tribal court exercised jurisdiction over lawsuits initiated by non-Indians against Indians arising on the reservation, "to allow the exercise of State jurisdiction here would undermine the authority of the Tribal courts over reservation affairs and hence would infringe on the right of Indians to govern them-selves".[32]

---

[31]The United States Environmental Protection Agency (EPA). Office of Water. American Indian Environmental Office. "Indian Training Program: Working Effectively with Tribal Governments." Participant Manual/Interim Final. U.S. Environmental Protection Agency Training Seminar. Aug. 1996, citing *Williams v. Lee,* 358 U.S. 217 (1959).
[32]*Id.*

The Supreme Court in the 1978 case *Santa Clara Pueblo v. Martinez* ruled that Native American tribes are dependent associations with limited powers of self-government.[33] Indian tribes possess limited sovereignty, but Congress may subject tribes to federal law where they expressly indicate and tribal sovereignty does not limit the effect of that law.

Conclusion[34]

The Supreme Court's rulings on tribal sovereignty have attempted to clarify the vagueness of the Constitution in defining tribal jurisdiction and self-government.

---

[33]*Santa Clara Pueblo v. Martinez*, 436 U.S. 49 (1978), as cited by Decker, Mary J. and Uram, Charlotte. "Jurisdiction Over Water Quality." *The Journal of Natural Resources* & *Environmental Law.* Vol. 8. No.1. 1992-1993.

[34]This conclusion is focused on *Williams v. Lee,* 358 U.S. 217 (1959); *Lone Wolf v. Hitchcock,* 187 U.S. 553 (1903); *Cherokee Nation v. Georgia,* 30 U.S. 1 (1831), unless otherwise noted.

The Court has generally held that tribes have restricted powers of self-government because of their dependency on Congress for the administration of their lands and resources. States' also may not interfere with tribal jurisdiction.

However, the Supreme Court when ruling on questions of Native American sovereignty and the jurisdiction of natural resources, land use, water rights, the regulation of hunting and fishing, etc., has been more inconsistent.

The Supreme Court has defined Native American sovereignty fairly consistently, and the executive and legislative branches of government have recognized the need to uphold sovereignty and self-determination. However, in practice the application of the concepts of Native American sovereignty for the departments and agencies responsible for management of tribal lands and resources has proven to be far more difficult and problematic.

Native American Sovereignty in the Executive and Legislative Branches of the US Government[35]

Historically, Native Americans have held a very distinctive position in the United States. Traditionally, the relationship between the U.S. and Native American Tribes has been a "government-to-government" relationship.[36] Tribes have been recognized as being sovereign entities that are capable of self-government. However, SSO tribes have been acknowledged to have a dependent status within the United States. Today, the federal government recognizes SSO Tribes that have distinctive legal rights and sovereign governmental powers.[37] These unique tribal powers are outlined in the Handbook of Federal Indian Law and rely on three principles,

---

[35]U.S.C. Title 25–Indians. Chapter 14--Miscellaneous. Subchapter II--Indian Self-Determination and Education Assistance; and U.S.C. Title 25--Indians. Chapter 14 Miscellaneous. Subchapter II--Indian Self-Determination and Education Assistance. Part A–Indian Self-Determination. Jan 16. 1996, unless otherwise noted.

[36]Bureau of Indian Affairs. Indian Education Program. "General Native American Information." April 29. 1996.

[37]*Id.*

(1) [A]n Indian tribe possesses, in the first instance, all the powers of any sovereign state; (2) [C]onquest renders the tribe subject to the legislative power of the United States and, in substance terminates the external powers of sovereignty of the tribe, for example, its power to enter into treaties with foreign nations, but does not by itself affect the internal sovereignty of the tribe; and (3) [T]hese powers are subject to qualification by treaties and by express legislation of Congress. Save as expressly qualified, full powers of internal sovereignty are vested in Indian tribes and in their duly constituted organs of government.[38]

The Handbook of Federal Indian Law outlines how the federal government currently defines Native American sovereignty.

---

[38]Handbook of Federal Indian Law. Felix S. Cohen, 1941.

In 1970, President Nixon announced a policy of self-determination for Native Americans, which was refined by the Reagan-Bush Administration in 1983. President Bush, on June 14, 1991, issued an American Indian policy statement that reaffirmed the government-to-government relationship between Indian tribes and the Federal Government. This relationship, according to the Bush-Quayle Administration, still allowed for tribes to assume the administration of federal health, natural resource, education, etc., programs based on the 1975 Indian Self-determination and Education Assistance Act.

In 1994, President Clinton in a "Memorandum For The Heads Of Executive Departments and Agencies" declared that the "U.S. Government has a unique relationship with Native American tribal governments as set forth in the Constitution of the United States, treaties, statutes, and court decisions."[39] According to Clinton, executive departments and agencies should design programs that are respectful of tribal sovereignty. Clinton, in his memorandum outlined several principles for executive departments and agencies to follow that promote a government-to-government relationship with federally recognized Native American tribes. President Clinton reaffirmed the position that the United States maintained with Indian tribes during the Nixon, Reagan, and Bush administrations.[40] In 2010 President Obama signed Tribal Law and Order Act of 2010, which further affirmed and expanded this relationship by allowing tribal authority to prosecute and

---

[39]White House Press Release. Memorandum For The Heads of Executive Departments and Agencies. "Government-to-Government Relations with Native American Tribal Governments." Office of the Press Secretary. 29 April 1994.
[40]*Id.*

punish criminals[41].

In 1973, Congress acknowledged that the assimilation/termination policy had been a failure. Congress then passed the Menominee Restoration Act in 1973 that rejected the termination policy. This statute brought the Menominee Tribe of Wisconsin federal recognition and "brought down the curtain on the termination era."[42]

---

[41]Tribal Law and Order Act. Fact Sheet. Department of Justice. 2018. https://www.justice.gov/tribal/tribal-law-and-order-act.

[42]Charles F. Wilkinson. "The Quest to Enforce the Old Promises: Indian Law in the Modern Era." *The Native American Rights Fund (NARF) Legal Review.* Special Edition: 15th Anniversary. NARF 1970-1985. Summer 1985.

The 1975 Indian Self Determination and Education Assistance Act, which found that the federal domination of Indian service programs had retarded rather than enhanced tribal realization of self government by failing to develop leadership skills within Indian communities. The Act also recognized that Native Americans would never surrender their desire to control relationships among themselves and with other non-Indian governments, organizations and people. The 1975 Act was ratified to strengthen tribal governments by authorizing the Indian Health Service (IHS) and Bureau of Indian Affairs (BIA) to contract out to Tribal governments most of the services that these agencies administer. Congress amended the Indian Self Determination and Education Act in 1988 and 1990, to include a declaration of commitment by the United States government. This declaration attempts to align the goals of the executive and legislative branches of government. Under the declaration,

Congress declares its commitment to the maintenance of the Federal government's unique and continuing relationship with, and responsibility to, individual Indian tribes and to the Indian people as a whole through the establishment of a meaningful Indian self determination policy which will permit an orderly transition from the Federal domination of programs for, and services to, Indians to effective and meaningful participation by the Indian people in the planning, conduct, and administration of those programs and services.[43]

The federal government also indicates, however, that in awarding self-determination contracts, or grants to tribes that,

(A)In general.--The United States reaffirms the trust responsibility of the United States to the [fill in name] Indian tribe(s) to protect and conserve the trust resources of Indian tribe(s) and the trust resources of individual Indians.[44]

---

[43]U.S.C. Title 25–Indians. Chapter 14--Miscellaneous. Subchapter II--Indian Self-Determination and Education Assistance; and U.S.C. Title 25--Indians. Chapter [14]Miscellaneous. Subchapter II–Indian Self-Determination and Education Assistance. Part A–Indian Self-Determination. Jan 16. 1996.
[44]*Id.*

One example of tribal resources that the United States has a trust responsibility for are the Indian forestlands.[45] Trust services to individual Indians involve services that only pertain to land or financial management connected to individually held allotments. The self-determination policy for tribes (that Congress has made a commitment to) is still contingent on the United States maintaining its trust responsibility for resources and Indian lands.

The 1988 Tribally-Controlled Schools Act of 1988 provides tribes the opportunity to manage Tribal Self-Governance Projects.[46] The Act allows tribes to create linguistic, cultural, and educational programs that fit the needs of their people.

---

[45]U.S.C. Title 25–Indians. Chapter 23–National Indian Forest Resources Management. Jan 16. 1996.
[46]The United States Environmental Protection Agency (EPA). Office of Water. American Indian Environmental Office. "Indian Training Program: Working Effectively with Tribal Governments." Participant Manual/Interim Final. U.S. Environmental Protection Agency Training Seminar. Aug. 1996, citing *Williams v. Lee*, 358 U.S. 217 (1959).

On October 4th, 1992, Congress enacted the Indian Environmental General Assistance Program Act.[47] The Act was amended on November 24th, 1993 to extend the authorization of the act until 1998. The Indian Environmental General Assistance Program Act specifically,

> Responds to the needs identified by Indian tribes for increased federal assistance to improve environmental protection on Indian lands. The Act authorizes the EPA to award multimedia grants, at a minimum of $75,000 per year, to Indian tribes to develop the necessary technical, legal and administrative infrastructure for effective environmental regulation.[48]

The Act was reauthorized on October 2, 1996 and is consistent with the Federal policies of Tribal Self-Determination and Self-Governance and EPA's 1984 Indian Policy Statement.

---

[47]Calendar No. 544. 104th Congress Report. Senate 2nd Session. 104-338. To Reauthorize the Indian Environmental General Assistance Program Act of 1992, and for Other Purposes. Committee on Indian Affairs. [To accompany S. 1834]. July 29. 1996, citing P.L. 102497, 106 Stat. 3258, 42 U.S.C. 4368B.
[48]*Id.*, citing P.L. 104-223.

Conclusion[49]

Respecting Native American sovereignty has become a critical part of both the policies of the executive and legislative branches of the United States government. Executive memorandums from the Nixon, Reagan, Bush, Clinton and Obama administrations have all reaffirmed the need to establish a policy of self-determination for tribes, and a government-to-government relationship in negotiations with them. President Trump has done very little with respect to Native American policy.

Congress has enacted most current legislation with provisions to recognize the federal government's self-determination and self-governance policies for tribes. However, the federal government has not relinquished its trust responsibilities for the management of tribal resources and land allotments.

---

[49]This conclusion is focused on General Native American Information. Indian Education Program. Bureau of Indian Affairs. April 29. 1996; and White House Press Release. Memorandum For The Heads of Executive Departments and Agencies. "Government-to-Government Relations with Native American Tribal Governments." Office of the Press Secretary. 29 April 1994, unless otherwise noted.

Additionally, because the federal government still provides grant and contract funds for tribal programs through departments and agencies, complete economic self-sufficiency has not yet been realized for all tribes.[50]

---

[50]U.S.C. Title 25--Indians. Chapter 14--Miscellaneous. Subchapter II--Indian Self-Determination and Education Assistance. Part A--Indian Self-Determination. Jan 16. 1996.

Balancing National Security Needs, Business and the Community's Right to Safe Drinking Water

Hawai'i Red Hill Fuel Facility

In 2014 the Red Hill Fuel Facility released 27,000 gallons of rocket fuel into Oʻahu's water table in which a judge ruled that the State of Hawaiʻi exemption violated the law.[51]

The Red Hill Fuel Facility has had multiple problems over the years which have necessitated that groundwater monitoring of the underlying basal aquifer and the PWC potable water source at Red Hill be conducted. The Red Hill Fuel tanks were fabricated in the 1940s. The tanks were originally constructed out of steel, which are corrosion prone over time, particularly with gradual exposure to salt.

---

[51]Associated Press. Judge: State's Exemption to Navy for Fuel Tanks Violated Law. February 22, 2018.
https://www.usnews.com/news/best-states/hawaii/articles/2018-02-22/judge-states-exemption-to-navy-for-fuel-tanks-violated-law.

Water contaminated by JP-5 and Diesel Fuel Marine rocket fuel is extremely toxic for consumption. Groundwater can contain *TPH GRO & DRO, BTXE, MTBE, PNAs, total lead (filtered), tetraethyl lead, and fractional analyses* after it is contained. 27,000 gallons of rocket fuel discharged into the water table has created a greater risk for epidemiological health risk, particularly in the elderly, children and pregnant women.

The problems have existed for over 15 years now. It is time for Pacific Command and the military to execute orders to complete replacement of the existing tanks with the construction of new alternatives (i.e. empty tanks) to allow maintenance on the ones being used. This is how electric utilities operate – they have a backup and alternative generator and are always making repairs on the system that is not in use. An Indefinite Demand Indefinite Quantity (IDIQ) and associated task orders can be issued to ensure that this is completed with adequate funding and in a timely fashion.

The servicemen and women and their families, in addition to the public at large on Oʻahu deserve clean water. Not having safe drinking water in of itself is a national security issue. It jeopardizes the health and well-being of America's servicemen and women and compromises their ability to lead effectively in the field.

This case highlights the need for the military to balance national security needs with the public's fitness and welfare; and right to clean water. This includes Native Hawaiʻians, Samoans and the other diverse populations throughout the islands.

Ensuring Businesses Compliance With Federal Law

Ineligible Uses of Federal Funds and a Community Health Center

Many HUD (and other federal) service and facility related programs that are designed to serve low- and moderate-income persons fail to meet the test or portions of a center or service are ineligible. This is important because Native Hawai'ians, Samoans and other families on O'ahu in many cases need these services. They add tremendous value to community, but only if they are meeting the program's objectives, not encouraging concurrent ineligible activities (i.e. for profit activities: day care, classes, et. al.) under the same facility's roof.

The project did not meet HUD's standards for eligibility and criteria for serving low- and moderate-income persons. The information outlined below details the specific areas of ineligibility.

A large percentage of the health center's facility square footage included administrative space - an item that was not eligible to receive HUD funding; and nearly 100% of the office space in in three separate buildings is used to lease space (on a permanent or intermittent basis) to private organizations that charge a fee and are not designed to serve low- and moderate-income persons.

Additionally this facility conducted church services (an *ineligible* activity). Four faith-based organizations were included in center's operations. It is ok for churches and other religious organizations to provide housing and services to the homeless but there are rigorous tests to meet the federal requirements to avoid discrimination based on race, gender and other protected classes.

Private commercial-for-profit enterprises that charge fees to their clients would be *cost-prohibitive* to low- and moderate-income persons. Including, but not limited to, $62.50 for 1.5 hour class of Irish Dance, $60 to $80 per hour (plus) for private Chiropractic services, karate lessons that are $50 per month, $400.00 +/- for the weightwatchers® program (that includes an annual fee that is required for participation in monthly meetings) and up to $100 in annual fees for the Hawaii Academy of Recording Arts. These activities by themselves are absolutely essential to small businesses development, but *not* for HUD programs. Instead the U.S. Chamber of Commerce and other business-related organizations could be tapped as sources of substantial grants and additional funding.

Board Meetings for Condo and Homeowners Associations are not HUD eligible activities when they are targeted on issues that pertain to those specific properties (and their property management) and are not providing services to low- and moderate-income persons. These condos are some of the most expensive real estate you can find in the United States.

Other miscellaneous activities that aren't applicable to low- and moderate-income persons included a Dreams & Health program. Yoga and other new-age activities are typically expensive and *not* eligible for federal funding because a Native Hawaiian or other low-income person may find the travel and program costs too expensive.

This health center also operates a childcare facility on the first floor of the one of the organization's buildings (5 plus) consisting of 5,794 square feet of space and charging up to $13,500 per child a year which is *cost-prohibitive* for low- and moderate-income persons (see specific detail on attached spreadsheet).

O'ahu's urban center is located on former marshlands; the area was originally dredged and filled. The beaches' white sand is imported. The State of Hawai'i even has a beach nourishment program. As a consequence the center's buildings are located in a flood plain and are at increased risk from flooding or a tsunami event.

Federal programs that are located in a floodplain require flood insurance. In accordance with this requirement the agency would be required to purchase flood insurance. The organization purchased flood insurance at the request of the City and County of Honolulu.

I requested that this organization provide information regarding the center's programs, in particular the childcare center; along with what were the residency breakdowns of the users of this service (% tourists, % urban area residents, % from others).

I also sought to get a better understanding of the current use of each building and requested receiving a list of its current tenants and the clientele that they serve through the organization's lease agreements.

Additionally I obtained information on any long-term tenants, including a list of community groups that use the facility on an intermittent basis, their clientele and any charges to use the facility if applicable. The following question was asked: Is there a selection process utilized regarding the lease/use of its facility?

This information requested resulted in a series of updates from the organization, detailing their tenants, beneficiaries, etc. (an extensive spreadsheet is provided detailing the particular uses of the facilities).

This spreadsheet provided specific evidence and documentation of the ineligible activities. The intent of many of these community-based organizations is admirable. However, if they don't meet the test for federal funding they should seek other types of grants and funding that are readily available.

This problematic situation of funding non-eligible activities based on a small percentage of a service or facilities eligibility is replicated throughout the United States and needs to be addressed.

Finally, the organization had already received funding to provide upgrades to the center and its associated facilities. For new funding the center would be required to identify and remediate any hazardous materials (lead based paint and asbestos) and complete any necessary relocation of tenants before work was initiated. The center responded in a June 3, 2011 letter that they would complete hazardous materials remediation *after* they finished the current project and at which time they would seek other federal funds.

The center sought a recommendation from an architect regarding HAZMAT remediation and required relocation. The City responded that they would be required to *first* complete any hazardous materials remediation and relocation - *not* afterwards. HAZMAT remediation is essential to worker safety.

Included is a asbestos insulation removal exercise in over 400 square feet in a basement with 18 inches of clearance as an example. This demonstrates the program safety equipment, including Dupont® Tyvek® suit with booties, goggles, safety glasses and full respirator.

Note this is *not* a sponsored endorsement of a specific brand by the author, only a recommendation to always wear the appropriate safety equipment. The author also used rubber gloves, although these are not shown in the subject photo.

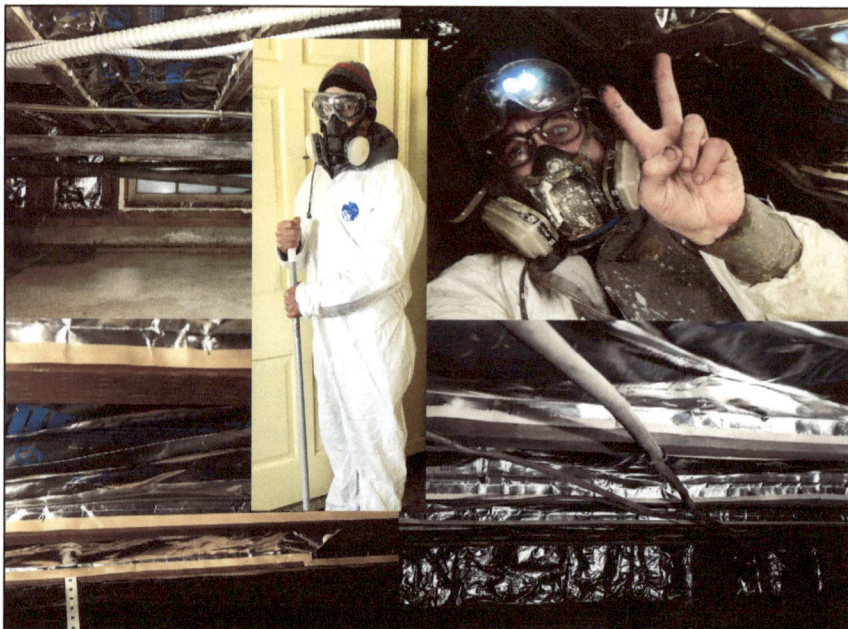

Matthew L. Myers showcasing Asbestos HAZMAT removal and remediation of an 18-inch +/- clearance basement (completed with replacement insulation).

Outlining proper HAZMAT and asbestos removal on a project site.

The cost involved in acquiring this safety equipment is approximately $50 dollars for the glasses, respirator, suit and gloves. There is no excuse for a project that receives millions of dollars in funding not to take this minor step. From a regulatory perspective the federal Occupational Safety and Health Administration (OHSA) requires that workers wear this type of remediation equipment, particularly on a federal project or service.

From a common sense viewpoint: Do you want to risk the health and safety of yourself, or your workers and/or staff?

No.

Corporations and not-for-profits lose billions of dollars in lost time due to medical injuries and long-term hospitalization. The time involved in taking the proactive safety precautions was less than 10 minutes for the photo above.

Reduced profitability and cost overruns from workers' compensation claims and other work-place related injuries impact all stakeholders, particularly shareholders. Asbestos and lead cause serious respiratory and developmental problems with long-term unprotected exposure.

There is no legitimacy in the argument that an apartment complex, affordable housing or community service that provides services to the public, particularly children, fails to test for lead paint and asbestos (and its binding agents), which are common in paint prior to 1950 and insulation.

It is almost a guarantee that a contractor, developer or service provider will find lead paint in older buildings. It has been banned since 1978. The same holds true for asbestos. It is a liability and should be remediated immediately and disposed of at an approved landfill.

Integrating Sustainability Into Corporate and Not-for-Profit Building Design

It is essential for modern corporations to design their programs and projects with sustainability in mind. It is not a cursory expense. For example, planning for erosion control on the upslope area above a commercial development or site prevents future site damage. The fire and flash flood prone areas in California and the western states (as mentioned previously); and coastal areas throughout the Continental U.S., Alaska and Hawai'i that are subject to hurricanes and tsunamis. Designing barriers that combine permeable and impermeable materials can be implemented well in advance if building on a vacant lot, repurposing an abandoned shopping mall or redeveloping existing structures.

Small expenditures in advance result in large insurance cost increase and damages later. Insurance companies benefit from lower premiums and small disaster payouts, improving the bottom line for shareholders and community-benefits for stakeholders. Downstream impacts to fisheries, factories, farms and other corporate entities are minimized because these entities do not have to filter their water supply to ensure continued production.

The site below is located in a mountainous region with 70 to 100 mile-per-hour gusts and only accessed by experienced pilots with training in multiple theatres. Flight suits, ear protection, communication helmets, boots (OSHA approved with steel toes) and safety equipment are essential. Heavy winds require being securely fastened to pilot and co-pilot seats and/or any passengers.

All participants understand the risks and liability and sign waivers, in addition to receiving training on being submerged under water (how to escape and free oneself) and crash-landing over land. Under no circumstances should recreational tourists venture into these types of areas without proper training and an experienced team.

The landing area, in this case required an exceptional pilot, experienced in landing under extremely challenging circumstances on a 25 square foot landing pad next to a sheer cliff with high risk of wind whiplash; and even crashing into the mountainside. Heavy fumes enter the helicopter and can make the occupants sick. Passengers with heart conditions or other respiratory issues should avoid travel like this.

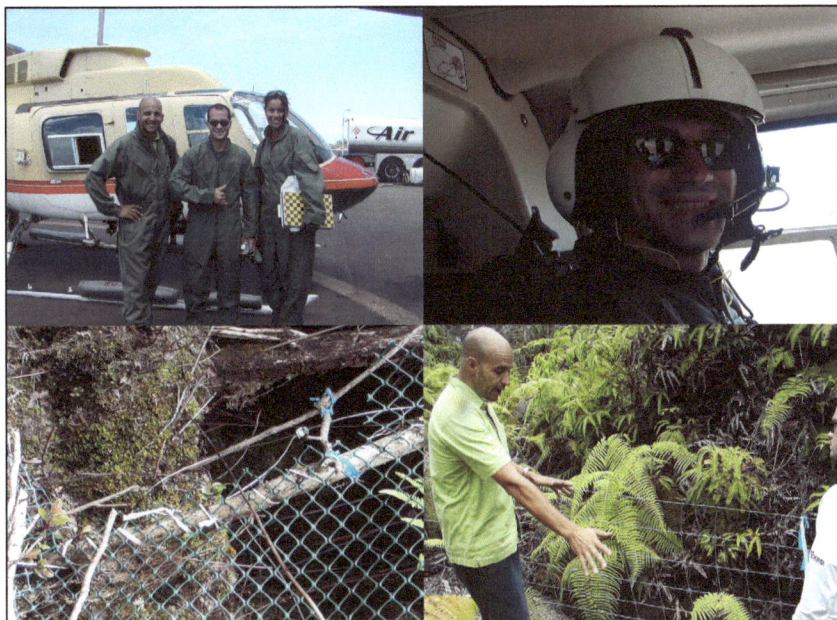
Team remote erosion control installation on undisclosed location.

This project illustrates how excellent erosion control starts in the mountains and continues down to coastal regions, creating a comprehensive and holistic approach to erosion control and proactive business development. This is the future of planning and should be implemented by municipalities, governments and corporations whenever possible.

Ensuring Clean Water With Legacy Public Works and Buildings

In Hawaiʻi and parts of the Continental U.S. there are still many legacy cesspool wastewater systems. These systems are inadequate, unsafe and impair businesses that surround them. On Oʻahu there are a still a number of businesses that utilize legacy cesspool systems. These systems have no lining and leach sewage and other pathogens directly in the water table, brackish and salt water systems, in addition to the ocean. They are bad for commerce, create hazardous conditions for tourists, fishermen surfers and divers, in addition to recreational swimmers. Children and the elderly are particularly vulnerable to waterborne illnesses.

In 2006 nearly 48 million gallons of sewage were discharged from a broken water main and had to be pumped into Oʻahu's Ala Wai Canal.[52] On February 22, 2018 9 million gallons of untreated sewage entered the Windward Oʻahu coast.[53] The losses for tourism in Hawaiʻi and businesses that rely of water for their production are large and reach multi-millions.

In California, farming operations use millions of gallons of diverted water in the Sacramento region for rice farming and other activities. The same is true for other water and wastewater systems. A septic tank (if new sewer lines can't be run due to logistical reasons) provides an appropriate level of protection in most cases.

---

[52]Robbie Dingeman. *Raw sewage spill largest in 20 years*. Honolulu Advertiser (now entitled StarAdvertiser). April 1, 2006.
[53]Allyson Blair, Reporter. During heavy rains, 9M gallons of sewage spilled in Windward Oahu. Hawaii News Now. February 22, 2018.

The Ka'a'awa beach house facilities are an excellent example of the type of systematic replacement cesspool systems on existing beach house facilities with new septic tanks, due to lack of sewer infrastructure along the Windward Coast of O'ahu.

Ka'a'awa beachhouse prior to replacement.

Kaʻaʻawa beach park area ahead of new facility improvements.

Facility upgrades included Americans with Disabilities (ADA) compliant parking, ADA access and new showers and bathrooms. Prior to this during heavy storm events the heavy rains would cause raw sewage to leach into the ocean. Persons in wheelchairs had difficulty entering the facility.

I was on Oʻahu for a storm that included 14 inches of rain in a 24 hour period. This caused heavy flooding and sewage discharge into the ocean, which makes the ocean too toxic to swim or surf in around Kaʻaʻawa and Punaluʻu. There is real value in systematically replacing facilities throughout the Hawaiʻian islands that have old cesspools.

Kaʻaʻawa Comfort Station Replacement

The proposed project was planned for the north end of Kaʻaʻawa Beach Park at the site of the existing comfort station. The bathhouse was a shower and bathroom station with a changing area for both men and women. The beach park is located at 51-329 Kamehameha Highway in Kaʻaʻawa, Oʻahu, Hawaiʻi. The park area is 65,340 square feet and is identified as TMK: (1) 5-1-002:025.

The existing comfort station was built in 1951 and consisted of an approximately 726 square feet concrete, tile, masonry and wood structure. The facility is used as a first stop from town for those traveling from windward Oʻahu and Honolulu to the north shore.

The City and County of Honolulu proposed to replace the existing comfort station at Kaʻaʻawa Beach Park with a new comfort station, replace existing wastewater treatment system and provide Americans with Disabilities Act (ADA) accessible parking and other miscellaneous site improvements. On Oʻahu, with the exception of military land and facilities, falls under the jurisdiction of the City and County of Honolulu (the entire island of Oʻahu is the County) and the State of Hawaiʻi.

The geology is flat along Kamehameha Highway and gradually tapers off toward the ocean with the exception of a drainage swale outlet between the existing comfort station and the northern property line. The project required excavation to demolish and remove the existing comfort station and wastewater system; and excavation for the new wastewater treatment system. The new bathhouse is now located at the site of the existing comfort station and parking lot. Excavation was also required for the footings and utilities; and grading was minor.

Proposed Use

The new structure is an 837 square feet concrete masonry structure with a wood framed 6 in 12 sloped standing seam metal roof. The design included bathrooms for men and women, changing rooms, park keeper's storage room; and an additional storage room, projecting roof eaves affording weather protection to access and ventilation penetrations and shower.

The building was constructed on the same location where the existing comfort station and parking was located. When you drive past the facility now it is a huge visual improvement and not as run-down inside. The grounds included top-dressing and re-grassing the areas surrounding the bathhouse with naupaka and grass, with no mitigation measures were necessary.

Summary of Comments

The State of Hawaiʻi, Department of Land and Natural Resources (DLNR) consulted the following City and County of Honolulu agencies for the beach house replacement: the Department of Planning & Permitting. The application was also referred to the State of Hawaiʻi agencies, including the Department of Land and Natural Resources divisions of Aquatic Resources, Forestry and Wildlife, Conservation and Resource Enforcement, Historic Preservation, Engineering, and the Land Division's Oahu District Land Office; the Department of Health; and the Office of Hawaiian Affairs.

Historic Significance of the Site and Archaeological Mitigation

The project was submitted on July 24, 2003, and provided the following comments, noting that no significant historic sites were found during an archeological inventory survey conducted for this project.

The State of Hawai'i Historic Preservation Division (SHPD) accepted the resulting archeological report including the recommendation for an on-site archeological monitoring for all ground disturbing activities.

This is not always the case for projects that involve more significant digging in Hawai'i in the low-lying coastal regions. Native Hawai'ians often buried ancestors in these low-lying areas. In is critical for projects to stop digging if they find human remains. It is also the law.

Archeological monitoring was recommended to mitigate any adverse effect ground disturbance on subsurface cultural deposits, including human burials. Archeological monitoring and preparation of an acceptable archeological monitoring plan was also required. This is standard practice throughout the Hawai'ian islands.

The archeological monitoring plan was submitted for review and acceptance near the completion of the permitting process. Typically no ground disturbing activities will take place until the plan is approved. This was the case in this project.

In addition to being a regulatory requirement, an archaeological monitoring plan is a common sense practice. Communities are naturally upset when a cemetery or military remains are disturbed. The same is true for indigenous cultures. It is important to respect burial grounds. It is also a regulatory requirement.

Review of Aquatic Impacts

The Ka'a'awa beach house facilities were not expected to have significant impacts adverse to aquatic resource values from the proposed bathhouse replacement. The site improvements clearly enhanced public facilities for beach visitors and motorists at the park. The site no longer has broken bathrooms, tile and leaking showers.

All construction activities occurred mauka of the park's certified shoreline Safeguards were taken to prevent debris, landscaping chemicals, eroded soil, petroleum products, untreated sewage and wastewater and other potential contaminants from flowing or leaching into coastal waters.

All construction activities occurred mauka of the park's certified shoreline.

It is a standard practice in Hawai'i to certify the location of the shoreline in order to establish a boundary between private and public ownership and access to the beach. This is due in part due to conflicts that arise out of the construction of seawalls and unauthorized piers that require permits.

Disputes in Hawai'i typically arise over exact boundaries and occur between shorefront landowners, the state; and in some cases, the federal government. This is due to the close proximity of properties in the area and the extremely high value of real estate for taxation purposes for the City and County of Honolulu. Shoreline properties range in the millions to tens of millions when they are offered for re-sale.

Control of Fugitive Dust

There is a significant potential for fugitive dust emissions during all phases of construction. The proposed construction activities occur in close proximity to existing residences, public areas and major thoroughfares, thereby exacerbating potential dust problems. A dust control management was required to be developed which identifies and addresses all activities that have a potential to generate fugitive dust. Implementation of adequate dust control measures during all phases of development and construction activities is warranted. Excessive construction dust causes damage to other properties and can cause respiratory problems for near by residents and business owners. It is a good practice to have in place from a practical perspective and is a regulatory requirement.

For example, construction activities must comply with all provisions of Hawaii Administrative Rules, §11-60.1-33 on Fugitive Dust. The contractor had to provide adequate measures to control dust from the road areas and during the various phases of construction.

The work activities had to plan for the different phases of construction, focusing on minimizing the amount of dust-generating materials and activities, centralizing on-site vehicular traffic routes, and locating potential dust-generating equipment in area of the least impact. An adequate water source was identified at the site prior to the start-up of construction activities. Landscaping provided rapid coverage of bare areas, including slopes, starting from the initial grading phase.

A best effort to minimize dust from shoulders and access roads was required. Additionally, the project included providing adequate dust control measures during weekends, after hours, and prior to daily start-up of construction activities. Controlling dust generated from debris being hauled away from the project site was also required. This is a common sense measure in addition to be legal requirement. No one wants to walk around a construction side, particularly on the windy Windward Oʻahu with sand, dust and dirt hitting residents and visitors.

The construction plans met all of the project requirements for fugitive dust, including erecting a fence with black dust control tarps (with minor incisions) to allow wind to travel through and dust control synthetic fabric to being completely torn off the fence.

Public Health Considerations

As there was no City and County of Honolulu sewer system in the vicinity plans were submitted and approved for the construction and use of a septic tank and soil absorption bed.

All wastewater plans had to conform to applicable provisions of the Department of Health's Administrative Rules, Chapter 11-62, Wastewater Systems. This rule includes provisions on how wastewater must be managed and is typical of any U.S. State, with an emphasis on Hawai'i's exposure to the ocean. Most of the rules and regulations are practical. Government can't allow public exposure to dangerous pathogens and other bacteria. This type of exposure can cause serious illness of even death; or even contribute to contagious waterborne viruses.

The following project requirements included a Special Management Area Use Permit – Major and a Shoreline Setback Variance was required for the project. A current certified shoreline survey (within one year of the application date) was required at the time the variance application was submitted. The Environmental Assessment (EA) required further clarification on whether the leach field was underground or aboveground. It was determined that the leech field was underground.

The EA had to address the effect of the leach field on coastal water quality. The EA required revision to discuss the feasibility of moving further away from the shoreline and/or putting the leaching field (if it is underground) underneath the parking area, to reduce the encroachment into the shoreline setback.

The EA had to report the impact of water run off from the outdoor shower facility on coastal water quality.

The quantity of grey water from the shower was relatively minimal and would be filtered by the beach sand before reaching the coastal groundwater and eventually migrating to coastal waters, where the dilution would be extremely large.

Other requirements included providing the square footage of the proposed facility, which was determined to be approximately 837 square feet. The area was not known for extensive seismic activity and was located in Seismic Zone 2A. Any excavation of the area would require a grading permit.

The applicant had to address the feasibility of compliance with flood requirements for this project. Although an exemption exists for this type of facility, every effort should be made at the planning and design stage to protect the city's (sizable) investment on this project from potential losses due to flooding.

The proposed individual wastewater system, including an underground septic tank and leach field, was designed and constructed in accordance with Hawaii Administrative Rules (HAR), Title 11, Department of Health, Chapter 62 – Wastewater Systems. The effluent from the individual wastewater systems (HAR §11-62) did not permit moving the proposed comfort station further away from the shoreline. HAR §11-62-32 requires that the septic tank and leach field be located a minimum horizontal distance of 50-feet from the shoreline. In this case, the majority of the proposed parking lot will be within the 50-feet shoreline setback, with adequate space under the proposed parking lot to install the septic tank and leach field.

Construction of a parking lot over a leach field, which consists of moist porous soil, and the parking lot, which requires a well-compacted sub-base to provide long-term, uniform structural support.

These are practical measures. Water flows over different types of materials and across different slopes at difference speeds. Rock or gravel allows water to enter the ground rapidly. Pavement causes water to runoff down site very differently. There are advantages and disadvantages to the use of different types of materials. Salt water and air are very corrosive immediately wearing even asphalt and concrete.

Finally, the existing ground in the vicinity of the proposed comfort station is approximately 7-feet above mean sea level (msl). To comply with the requirements of the special flood hazard district, the finish floor and lowest horizontal structural member was constructed above the base flood elevation of 10-feet above msl. This would required a long and extensive ramp to provide accessibility and meet the requirements of the American with Disabilities Act (ADA).

Hawai'i Conservation District Requirements

The purpose of the conservation district on O'ahu, Hawai'i is to conserve, protect, and preserve the important natural resources of the State through appropriate management to promote their long-term sustainability and the public health, safety, and welfare. For example for this specific project, the identified land use was as follows: Section 13-5-22, Hawaii Administrative Rules (HAR), Identified land uses in the protective subzone, P-9 Structures, Existing, C-1, requires demolition removal, or alteration of existing structures, facilities and equipment. The existing comfort station is being demolished and replaced with a new City and County of Honolulu Prototype Bathhouse of similar size and in the same location. The land use will not change.

The proposed land use was consistent with the objectives of the Subzone of the land on which the use will occur. The land is located in the General (G) Subzone, per HAR §13-5-14. "The objective of this subzone is to provide for areas processing unique developmental qualities which complement the natural resources of the area." The project consisted of the replacement of an existing structure. The use did not change.

The beach station also complied with the provisions and guidelines contained in Chapter 205A, HRS entitled "Coastal Zone Management", where applicable. The land use conforms to Chapter 205A-2: to provide adequate, recreational opportunities in the coastal zone management through a sufficient supply of shoreline parks and other recreational facilities.

The construction did not have a adverse impact to the natural resources of the area. The exact opposite was the case: the project removed a dangerous cesspool system and replaced it with a septic tank and ADA facilities, a substantial improvement from the previous dilapidated state that generated an elevated risk of pathogens in the ocean surrounding the facility.

The State of Hawai'i and the City and County of Honolulu have specific zones in which certain types of activities are permitted (residential, commercial, industrial, et. al.). This is typical of any state in the United States. Each state has unique rules and regulations and engages in a different method of land use permitting. The replacement of the comfort station did not change the current land use. The land use, including buildings, structures and facilities, was compatible with the locality and surrounding areas.

The project had a negligible and minimally impact on the scenic views of the ocean compared to the existing condition. The Kamehameha highway elevation of the existing comfort station included the following dimensions: 37′ wide and the roof is 12′ at its peak and 27′ wide. The roof started 8′ with the hip roof peak at 17′. Ocean views remain around to each side of the proposed structure. The visual characteristics of the existing beach park remained unchanged except for the additional height of the new bathhouse hip roof. The project was a vast improvement over the old one. The bathroom fixtures were no longer broken and corroded. The existing comfort station and parking lot had been in extremely poor condition.

The project benefited the community surrounding the beach park, and residents and tourists traveling from windward Oʻahu and Honolulu to the North Shore[54] by providing them with a clean modern replacement for the current dilapidated and accessibility restricted comfort station.

---

[54]The consultant for the applicant noted "the comfort station has always been highly utilized as a first stop from town for those traveling from windward Oahu and Honolulu to the north shore."

Due to the extreme closeness of the facility to the ocean the City and County of Honolulu typically recommends for similar net new projects that structures which are located in an area that are subject to coastal erosion, be demolished, rebuilt and located away from the beach and shoreline. However, in this case the project was approved and is still standing.

Business Impacts of Facility Improvements.

No resident or tourist wants to swim in dirty water, particularly water contaminated by raw sewage and construction runoff. The costs for losses to tourism in Hawai'i run in the tens to hundreds of millions. Replacing a bathhouse and cesspool is a simple fix, costing several hundred thousand. The liability of a resident or tourists becoming sick and hospitalized from health concerns is very high for the City and County of Honolulu and the State of Hawai'i. The benefits outweigh the costs for business and the State. The same is true on the U.S. mainland.